LESSONS IN T

PHONICS

IN PRIMARY SCHOOLS

DAVID WAUGH, JANE CARTER
AND CARLY DESMOND

Los Angeles | London | New Delhi
Singapore | Washington DC

Learning Matters
An imprint of SAGE Publications Ltd
1 Oliver's Yard
55 City Road
London EC1Y 1SP

SAGE Publications Inc.
2455 Teller Road
Thousand Oaks, California 91320

SAGE Publications India Pvt Ltd
B 1/I 1 Mohan Cooperative Industrial Area
Mathura Road
New Delhi 110 044

SAGE Publications Asia-Pacific Pte Ltd
3 Church Street
#10-04 Samsung Hub
Singapore 049483

Editor: Amy Thornton
Development editor: Geoff Barker
Production controller: Chris Marke
Project management: Swales & Willis Ltd,
Exeter, Devon
Marketing manager: Lorna Patkai
Cover design: Wendy Scott
Typeset by: C&M Digitals (P) Ltd, Chennai, India
Printed by: CPI Group (UK) Ltd, Croydon, CR0 4YY

Library of Congress Control Number: 2015940818

British Library Cataloguing in Publication Data

A catalogue record for this book is available from
the British Library

ISBN 978-1-4739-1593-0
ISBN 978-1-4739-1594-7 (pbk)

Contents

The authors   vi
Acknowledgements   vii

Introduction   viii

1 Why phonics?   1

2 Phonics in context   14

3 Reception: Developing phonemic awareness   27

4 Reception: Beginning to read and write using CVC words   38

5 Year 1: Teaching grapheme–phoneme correspondences   49

6 Year 1: Long vowel digraphs   64

7 Year 1: Decoding and encoding text   75

8 Years 1 and 2: Morphemes – prefixes, suffixes and root words   85

9 Year 2: Homophones and contractions   99

10 Year 2: Phonics into spelling   114

11 Teaching tricky or common exception words   126

12 Moving on   142

Glossary   157
Index   160

The authors

David Waugh is subject leader for Primary English at Durham University. He has published extensively in Primary English. David is a former deputy head teacher, was Head of the Centre for Educational Studies at the University of Hull, and was Regional Adviser for ITT for the National Strategies from 2008 to 2010. As well as his educational writing, David also writes children's stories, including *Lottie's Run* published in 2015.

Jane Carter's teaching experience includes 20 years in local primary schools as a teacher, deputy head and then local authority consultant, before joining the University of the West of England to focus on Initial Teacher Education. She now combines her time at UWE with managing a Teaching School Alliance. Her passion is the teaching of English and in particular engaging children through children's literature and motivating children as writers. Jane's research concentrates on the teaching of reading and includes a European-wide children's literature project.

Carly Desmond is an assistant head teacher at Flamstead End School. Her particular interest lies within phonics and early reading. In her role as literacy leader she has successfully supported staff in the training, planning and modelling of phonics lessons. This has led to successful phonic screening scores. Flamstead End School was also recently graded outstanding by OFSTED.

LESSONS IN TEACHING PHONICS IN PRIMARY SCHOOLS

Acknowledgements

Every effort has been made to trace the copyright holders and to obtain their permission for the use of copyright material. The publisher and author will gladly receive any information enabling them to rectify any error or omission in subsequent editions.

The authors are grateful to all the teachers and trainee teachers who shared ideas and case studies.

Introduction

This book focuses on teaching and learning systematic synthetic phonics in Reception, Year 1 and Year 2, with additional attention given to the needs of Key Stage 2 children who have yet to master phonics at the required level. There is a popular misconception that all teaching of early reading revolves solely around the development of children's phonic knowledge. The English National Curriculum Objectives for Year 1 certainly emphasise phonic knowledge strongly. Look at the statutory requirements for word reading for Year 1.

Word reading:

- apply phonic knowledge and skills as the route to decode words;

- respond speedily with the sound to graphemes for all 40+ phonemes, including, where applicable, alternative sounds for graphemes;

- read accurately by blending sounds in unfamiliar words containing grapheme–phoneme correspondences (GPCs) that have been taught;

- read common exception words, noting unusual correspondences between spelling and sound and where these occur in the word;

- read words containing taught GPCs and *-s*, *-es*, *-ing*, *-ed*, *-er* and *-est* endings;

- read other words of more than one syllable that contain taught GPCs;

- read words with contractions [for example, *I'm*, *I'll*, *we'll*], and understand that the apostrophe represents the omitted letter(s);

- read aloud books that are consistent with their developing phonic knowledge and that do not require them to use other strategies;

- re-read these books to build up their fluency and confidence in word reading.

(DfE, 2013, p20)

However, on the next page, the National Curriculum also emphasises comprehension.

Develop pleasure in reading, motivation to read, vocabulary and understanding by:

- listening to and discussing a wide range of poems, stories and non-fiction at a level beyond that at which they can read independently;

- being encouraged to link what they read or hear read to their own experiences;

- becoming very familiar with key stories, traditional tales, retelling them and considering their particular characteristics;

- recognising and joining in with predictable phrases;

- learning to appreciate rhymes and poems, and to recite some by heart;

- discussing word meanings, linking new meanings to those already known.

Understand both the books they can already read accurately and fluently and those they listen to by:

- drawing on what they already know or on background information and vocabulary provided by the teacher;

- checking that the text makes sense to them as they read and correcting inaccurate reading;

- discussing the significance of the title and events;

- making inferences on the basis of what is being said and done;

- predicting what might happen on the basis of what has been read so far;

- participating in discussion about what is read to them, taking turns and listening to what others say;

- explaining clearly their understanding of what is read to them.

(DfE, 2013, p21)

Teaching phonics is not an alternative to teaching comprehension and developing children's love of reading; it is an integral part of that process. It is important to remember this and constantly to keep in mind that learning phonics is a means to an end (good reading) rather than an end in itself. In this book, we examine what is needed to develop phonic knowledge and understanding, but we emphasise that this knowledge and understanding needs to develop alongside reading comprehension so that children are not only able to read by decoding words, but are also interested in and engaged by reading.

Chapters include activities, where appropriate, to enable you to check on your growing subject knowledge. We have also suggested further reading to help you to develop your understanding, and resources and websites that will support your work in the classroom.

In Chapter 1, we look closely at the teaching of reading and the place of phonics, providing some historical perspectives and demonstrating why it is so important that we teach reading well.

Chapter 2 places phonics firmly in the classroom context and provides a range of strategies for developing an environment in which children can learn successfully.

Chapters 3 to 10 provide lesson ideas and plans with clear explanations and guidance on subject knowledge needed for successful teaching and learning. Each lesson is placed in context and suggestions are provided for developing further lessons to take children's learning forward. Because we are aware that schools and teacher training institutions have different ways of planning, we have tried to vary the format for lesson plans to show a variety of approaches.

Chapter 11 examines the anomalies in the English alphabetic system that can sometimes make teaching and learning phonics challenging. The chapter examines 'tricky' or 'common exception' words and ways in which we can help children to learn these.

Our final chapter, 'Moving on', looks at ways in which what has been studied in the previous chapters can be developed in a language-rich environment.

At the end of the book you will find a glossary of key terminology.

We hope that this book will help you to develop your subject knowledge for teaching reading and that it will provide you with ideas and strategies which will enhance your teaching and, most importantly, children's learning.

David Waugh

Jane Carter

Carly Desmond

2015

Reference

Department for Education (DfE) (2013) *The National Curriculum in England: Framework Document*. London: DfE.

Why phonics?

Teachers' Standards

Working through this chapter will help you meet the following standards:

3. Demonstrate good subject and curriculum knowledge:

- Have a secure knowledge of the relevant subject(s) and curriculum areas, foster and maintain pupils' interest in the subject, and address misunderstandings.
- Demonstrate a critical understanding of developments in the subject and curriculum areas, and promote the value of scholarship.
- Demonstrate an understanding of and take responsibility for promoting high standards of literacy, articulacy and the correct use of standard English, whatever the teacher's specialist subject.
- If teaching early reading, demonstrate a clear understanding of systematic synthetic phonics.

Introduction

It is clear from the Teachers' Standards above that the teaching of systematic synthetic phonics has a high priority in terms of the knowledge and understanding required to meet the Standards. There are no other examples in the Standards where a particular approach to teaching is stipulated, and so clearly the reasons behind this emphasis and priority require some discussion and explanation.

Why the focus on the teaching of reading?

The impetus for developing effective teaching of reading practice is found in the evidence that tells us that being a reader is an indicator of future socio-economic success (OECD, 2002) and that motivated readers who read for pleasure and purpose are also more likely to be higher attaining readers who achieve wider academic success (DfE, 2012). Neil Gaiman, a highly regarded children's (and adults') author, addressed the Reading Agency Conference in 2014 and shared an experience he had in America. He said:

> *I was once in New York, and I listened to a talk about the building of private prisons – a huge growth industry in America. The prison industry needs to plan its future growth – how many cells are they going to need? How many prisoners are there going to be, 15 years from now? And they found they could predict it very easily, using a pretty simple algorithm, based about asking what percentage of ten and eleven year olds couldn't read. And certainly couldn't read for pleasure.*

There is no debate about the need to get the teaching of reading right for all children: the debate focuses around the question of how this can become a reality. This debate has been termed the 'reading wars', due to the ferocious nature of arguments and the fervently held beliefs on all sides. To the student teacher, this appears like a rather complex picture and, yes, reading is a complex business, but if we are clear about the ultimate aim of a teacher of reading it becomes possible to build the picture, based on the research evidence, of the approaches and strategies that will support all children in becoming readers.

What is reading?

What comprises 'reading' and the 'best way' to teach reading are perhaps the most intense areas of debate that have consumed educationalists over many years. The words here give us a clue to the breadth and depth of the debate: what is meant by the 'best way' to teach reading and in fact, what do we understand by the term 'reading'? Does this mean the most effective in terms of children's word reading skills – so the child that can look at a word and say the word – or is 'reading' also about comprehension of what is read, both in terms of the individual words and comprehension across a sentence and a whole text?

It could also be argued that the approach taken to the teaching of reading needs to ensure that children also become self-motivated and engaged readers. Teachers often talk about the difference between children in their class who can 'read' and those who are 'readers' – the difference between children who can lift the words from the page and 'read them' compared to those who can do this *and* understand, engage and respond to those words *and* who can articulate their reading preferences *and* are able to make choices about their reading to match different purposes.

It is this final definition, with all its constituent parts, that we need to aim for as teachers of reading. These different elements of a reader are also found in the National Curriculum (DfE, 2013). It is helpful to look at the expectations of the curriculum at key points in a child's reading journey to understand what these elements of a reader might look like in practice and what we should teach to enable all children to become readers.

Reading in the curriculum

The statement in the new curriculum about reading gives a very clear message about the expectations for the outcomes of the approach taken to teach reading. It states that:

> All pupils must be encouraged to read widely across both fiction and non-fiction to develop their knowledge of themselves and the world in which they live, to establish an appreciation and love of reading, and to gain knowledge across the curriculum. Reading widely and often increases pupils' vocabulary because they encounter words they would rarely hear or use in everyday speech. Reading also feeds pupils' imagination and opens up a treasure-house of wonder and joy for curious young minds.
>
> It is essential that, by the end of their primary education, all pupils are able to read fluently, and with confidence, in any subject in their forthcoming secondary education.

(DfE, 2013, p4)

In addition to this, the curriculum organises the elements of reading into two areas: word reading and comprehension.

The National Curriculum gives the following overview of word reading (DfE, 2013, p13).

> Skilled word reading involves both the speedy working out of the pronunciation of unfamiliar printed words (decoding) and the speedy recognition of familiar printed words. Underpinning both is the understanding that the letters on the page represent the sounds in spoken words. This is why phonics should be emphasised in the early teaching of reading to beginners (i.e. unskilled readers) when they start school.

Phonics is identified here as the prime approach to the teaching of reading.

Activity: Elements of reading

Can you sort the following elements of reading (taken from the National Curriculum programmes of study) into 'word reading' or 'comprehension'?

- Link what children read or hear read, to their own experiences.
- Read accurately by blending the sounds in words.
- Check that the text makes sense as you read and correct inaccurate reading.
- Predict what might happen on the basis of what has been read so far.
- Read words containing common suffixes.
- Read accurately recognising alternative sounds for graphemes.

What is phonics?

Phonics is an approach to the teaching of early reading that involves the linking of spoken sounds to letters or groups of letters. Phonics is distinct from, but linked to *phonological awareness*. Phonological awareness is about the awareness of sounds and abilities to hear chunks of sound in the spoken word. Goswami (2010, p103) explains phonology as *the way the brain represents the sound structure of spoken language*. Jolliffe and Waugh with Carss (2012, p4) cite a range of research that demonstrates that from a young age babies and children are able to manipulate the sounds of language, even being able to orally blend the sounds in words into the words themselves. Playing with words, rhyming, manipulating sounds for effect, creating a rhythm, a poem or song, are all part of phonological awareness, and any visit to an Early Years setting will see practitioners and children enjoying and developing an awareness of sounds through story, song, rhymes and engaging with the natural environment. Goswami (2010) and many other researchers see the development of phonological awareness as a key stepping stone and supporting predictor of *phonemic awareness*. *Phonemic awareness is the conscious understanding that words are made up of individual sounds (phonemes) and that sounds are represented through the alphabet* (Farmer et al., 2006, p40).

It is worth remembering that reading is not really a natural process. After all, when the human race began, there were no written forms of the language in the way we would recognise today. Humans have invented a code that enables us to record what we say and to be able to read it back reliably. This invented code has developed and has its basis in the Roman alphabet. The English alphabet, while common to many languages, is distinct from other alphabets of the world and anyone who can read Greek or Russian will be aware of the huge differences. This linking of sounds to letters can be quite simple with certain alphabets. Spanish, for example, has 24 different speech sounds (Mora, 2001) that make up the spoken word and has the same 26 letters in the alphabet as we do, so it is a reasonably simple process of using the letters to represent the sounds. The Spanish use 29 different combinations of the letters to make the 21 different sounds they have for speaking, reading and writing.

Like many other languages, Spanish uses diacritical marks to change the way some letters are pronounced. These marks creep into our own language and you will be familiar with words such as *café* and know that the accent on the *e* changes the way it is pronounced. English, however, has 44 different speech sounds in its language, but we still have the same 26 letters of the alphabet to work with to represent these sounds. The challenge that our language brings, however, is not in the number of speech sounds we use but in the different combinations of letters we use to represent these sounds. We have over 150 common ways of representing those 44 sounds and over 400 possible ways, some of which only occur in a few words! The English language has evolved over the centuries, acquiring many words from other languages, which partly explains the wide range of speech sounds in the language. For example, Bald (2007, p50) explains that *roughly 30 percent of the most common words are of French origin.*

You will see in later chapters that the speech sounds are called 'phonemes' and the letter or letters that represent them, 'graphemes'. Phonics is therefore the process of linking phonemes and graphemes.

Approaches to teaching reading: An historical perspective

This part of the chapter will briefly review some of the differing methods for teaching reading and identify the role phonics teaching plays (or not) in these methods. We will also begin to address the research and the theoretical models that underpin these approaches.

The alphabetic method

Learning to read did not need to be of national concern back in medieval England; after all, most people did not learn to read or even need to learn to read! For those that did, the learning of the alphabet and the letter names (rather than the sounds of the letters) was the focus of the learning process. At this time, most reading and writing was in Latin and it wasn't until a little later in history that the reading of English was taught. For those who did learn to read, the 'hornbook' was used as one of the first reading resources. Today, we might go to the internet to find a pre-prepared PowerPoint or interactive white board flipchart page, but in the past a teacher would give a child a hornbook, which resembled a rectangular table tennis bat overlaid with the handwritten lesson to be learnt, often the alphabet or a religious text. Children could then refer to it at all times, as it was tied to their waist or hung around the neck. The letter names were learnt and children were taught to recognise the lower and upper case letters in the order they appeared in the alphabet.

The phonics approach

The alphabetic approach began to be superseded by the phonics approach sometime later. Where letter *names* had been learnt previously, the learning of the letter *sounds* became the preferred approach to the teaching of reading by the early nineteenth century. The complexity of the English language was addressed through the learning of syllable sounds as well. Over the next 100 years this phonics approach has been refined and revisited with different phonics approaches being used over time. Phonics is what is known as a 'sub-lexical' approach, meaning an approach that uses and pays attention to the constituent parts of a word, rather than a 'lexical' approach that focuses on the whole word. Two significant approaches to phonics teaching and learning are the 'analytic' and the 'synthetic' approaches and each uses sub-lexical knowledge in different ways.

Analytical phonics

The analytical approach is often described as a 'problem solving' approach, because it encourages children to make links between patterns of sound found in words. At its simplest level, it is about encouraging children to apply what they have learnt about the sounds in one word to other similar words and this might be termed 'analogy phonics', e.g. if I know how to read the word 'black' I can use the knowledge of the sound pattern 'ack' to help me read the words: back, lack, pack, quack, rack, sack, tack. Brooks (2003, p11) defines this approach as one

> in which the phonemes associated with particular graphemes are not pronounced in isolation. Children identify (analyse) the common phoneme in a set of words in which each word contains the phonemes under study.

Children are encouraged to deduce and infer as they read, using their prior word reading knowledge to inform the decoding process. This particular approach to phonics was popular at a time when the Plowden Report (1967) broadly advocated child-centred education, later followed by the Bullock Report (1975), which placed an emphasis on children as active learners, constructing their own knowledge. The analytical approach sits within these frameworks and understandings of children's learning.

Synthetic phonics

Synthetic phonics, as defined by Washtell (2010, p44), is *an approach to the teaching of phonics which works by isolating the phonemes in a word. The phonemes are then blended together in sequence to decode the word.* This approach is often characterised as a more systematic approach to the teaching of phonics than the analytical approach. Letter sound correspondences are introduced to children in a systematic and planned sequence and children are taught to 'synthesise' (hence the name synthetic phonics) the sounds to form words. This is the favoured approach in the National Curriculum (DfE, 2013) and has been the subject of high-level debate in many of the English speaking countries of the world, in particular the United States and Australia.

The whole word approach

This approach was evident in the teaching of reading in the 1940s and 1950s, although it can be traced as far back as 1908 when Edmund Huey, an American psychologist, promoted it. It is commonly known as the 'look and say' approach. Children were introduced to whole words (working at a lexical level) through a series of graded and progressive flash cards, often accompanied by a picture to link the reading of the word with its meaning. Children were taught to look carefully at words, noting their shapes and patterns and through this learning to say the whole word.

This approach was accompanied by graded readers which introduced vocabulary in a controlled and progressive way, giving children the opportunity to apply their whole word, sight vocabulary in context. Some children who were taught using this approach worked out for themselves the sub-lexical structures (including the phonic structures) and patterns of words and so were able to read unfamiliar words they encountered in new texts, but for many other children this approach left them without strategies to tackle new words.

The whole language approach

This approach sees reading as a meaning-driven endeavour and so embeds the teaching of reading within language as a whole. This is often seen as reading being taught through the act of reading; learning embedded in its context. There is a focus on immersing children in engaging and enjoyable texts and this enables the teacher to support children in learning and applying a range of reading skills. One key proponent of this approach, Ken Goodman (1967), famously described reading as *a psycholinguistic guessing game* that is a process of referring to prior knowledge in an attempt to make sense of and so decode what is being read. In the 1980s, some teachers favoured this approach, partly as a response to the feeling that the structured reading schemes on offer were having a detrimental effect on children's motivation and consequently their progress in reading. The whole language approach used phonics teaching incidentally and only where it was thought to be needed. This approach fell out of favour in the 1990s.

Activity: How did you learn to read?

- Can you remember how you were taught to read?
- Can you locate the method by which you were taught to read in the different methods outlined above?

Theoretical underpinnings

To understand these different approaches, it is helpful to recognise the different research perspectives that inform them. Kathy Hall, in her introduction to the book *Interdisciplinary Perspectives on Learning to Read* (2010, p3), lists some of the disciplines that have informed the debate: socio-cultural, semiotic, educational, linguistic, historical, political, psychological and neuro-scientific/biological traditions. You can tell from this list that not only is reading a complex issue, but also understanding the research that informs our understanding of reading is equally (if not more so) complex! In the next part of this chapter, two significant theoretical perspectives will be explored.

The orchestration models of reading

The 'orchestration models' of reading comprise one group of theoretical models relevant to the teaching of reading and phonics. These refer to psycholinguistic theoretical models that suggest that *strategic use of multiple sources of information is necessary in order to derive understanding from written texts* (Stuart *et al.*, 2008, p60). The 'Searchlights Model' of reading is an adaptation of this theoretical perspective and underpinned recent approaches to the teaching of reading as set out in the Primary National Strategy (DfEE, 1998). Figure 1.1 shows the different cueing systems that were identified (and so 'orchestrated') in the reading process: phonics; knowledge of context; grammatical knowledge and word recognition and graphic knowledge.

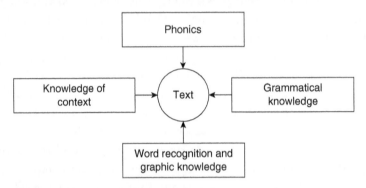

Figure 1.1 Different cueing systems identified in the reading process

The model suggested that teaching needed to guide children to use or orchestrate each of the different cueing systems – selecting the most appropriate and effective in each reading context.

While this model may look attractive as a representation of the different aspects of knowledge that the expert reader may draw on to read, researchers have suggested and generally agree that it does not adequately represent what beginner readers do (Stuart *et al.*, 2008). Not only this, it was argued that the model confused word reading and comprehension, suggesting that words could be 'read' by using comprehension strategies, e.g. working out an unknown word in a sentence by predicting what it could be from the context. This, it was argued, was not a reliable approach to word reading.

The Simple View of Reading model

A different theoretical model, the one that is embedded in the National Curriculum (2013), is called the 'Simple View of Reading'. This model was first put forward by Gough and Tunmer (1986), who – from a cognitive psychological research background – proposed that reading comprised two distinct processes: listening comprehension and decoding. They suggested that reading comprehension was a product of the combination of listening comprehension and decoding. Rose (2006) explained each dimension when adopting this model as the favoured approach in the *Independent Review of the Teaching of Early Reading* (2006, p37). He said:

> In this context, word recognition is the process of using phonics to recognise words. Language comprehension is the process by which word information, sentences and discourse are interpreted: a common process is held to underlie comprehension of both oral and written language.

The model was represented as a diagram (see Figure 1.2). This way of representing the model enables the teacher to 'plot' a child's reading skills and knowledge. A child who has excellent language comprehension but weak word recognition skills would be plotted in the left-hand, top quadrant of the diagram. This plotting exercise, it is suggested, is one way of reflecting on the learning needs of each child and therefore the emphasis of teaching needed, i.e. the child in the top left quadrant needs a greater teaching emphasis on word recognition skills and so further, targeted phonics teaching.

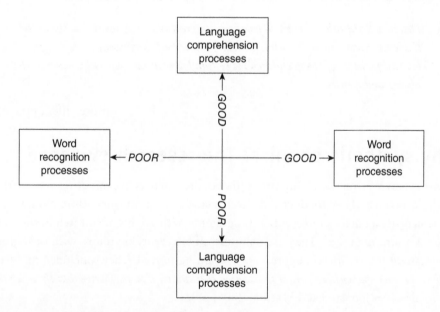

Figure 1.2   The Simple View of Reading (DfES, 2006, p53)

Activity: The Simple View of Reading

- As with all theoretical models, debate continues to surround reading and the 'Simple View of Reading'. For a range of contrasting perspectives read the journal *Literacy* (2008, vol. 2, no. 2). Particularly helpful is the article by Stuart *et al.* when read alongside, and in contrast to, the article by Kirby and Savage.
- Think about the skills and knowledge as readers of the children you have taught; can you plot them on the 'Simple View of Reading' model?

The *Independent Review of the Teaching of Early Reading* (2006)

With the complex and multifaceted approaches outlined above, it is perhaps not surprising that successive governments have attempted to direct the approaches taken to the teaching of reading. In recent times, the most significant and influential intervention has been the review commissioned by government and undertaken by Sir Jim Rose in 2006.

The Rose Report, as it is often referred to, was commissioned following reports to the House of Commons Select Committee on Education on their nominated topic of enquiry 'Teaching Children to Read' (Ellis and Moss, 2014). Rose reviewed research evidence from around the world, as well as drawing on evidence from practice in schools. He concluded that *systematic phonics work* taught in *discrete lessons* and embedded in a *rich curriculum that fosters all four interdependent strands of language: speaking, listening, reading and writing* should be implemented in schools. He also stated that:

> *Despite uncertainties in research findings, the practice seen by the review shows that the systematic approach, which is generally understood as synthetic phonics, offers the vast majority of young children the best and most direct route to becoming skilled readers and writers.*

> (Rose, 2006, pp3–4)

Why synthetic phonics? The research evidence

Johnston and Watson (2005) are two influential researchers in promoting systematic synthetic phonics. They conducted a research study in Clackmannanshire, Scotland, implementing a phonics intervention programme with groups of children in the early stages of learning to read. They had a number of intervention groups, with each group being taught using different approaches to learning to read. They concluded that *the synthetic phonics approach, as part of the reading curriculum, is more effective that the analytical phonics approach* (Johnston and Watson, 2005, p9).

It was this report that was cited by Rose (2006) and was significant in his conclusions and recommendations about the teaching of reading and phonics. The research methodology and thus the robustness of the findings has been contested, and in reaching your own conclusions it is useful to read widely. Wyse and Styles (2007), in an article titled 'Synthetic phonics and the teaching of reading: The debate surrounding England's "Rose Report"', provided a detailed critique of the study, which is then countered and critiqued in a series of articles in the journal *Literacy* (2007). These articles play out the debates surrounding the research and provide a good starting point for your own analysis of research evidence that you encounter.

A further area of debate surrounds the teaching of synthetic phonics to able readers and in particular children who begin school as readers. Davis (2013) highlights this debate in his article 'To read or not to read: Decoding synthetic phonics' and also challenges the research evidence that has been used to promote synthetic phonics. He challenges the assumption that successful phonics teaching can automatically be equated with the successful teaching of reading. Reading, he claims, is not simply about mastering letter–sound correspondences, but is about the making of meaning, and that while phonics can help some children on their journey to becoming readers it is not an approach that supports all children and, in particular, the able reader.

Conclusion

While there is a continuing debate about the type of phonics and how much phonics should be taught, there is agreement that phonics does have a significant role to play in the teaching of early reading (Lewis and Ellis, 2006). With this in mind, teachers need to be equipped with the subject knowledge and pedagogical skills to teach phonics as part of a reading programme in a way that is engaging, motivating and purposeful. The following chapters in this book will equip you to do this.

Learning outcomes review

You should now have an historical perspective of the role of phonics in the teaching of early reading. You should also be aware of some of the theoretical underpinnings for the teaching of early reading and phonics and an overview of some of the research evidence.

Answers to the elements of reading activity (page 3)
You were asked to sort the following elements of reading into 'word reading' or 'comprehension'.

- Link what children read or hear read, to their own experiences – comprehension

- Read accurately by blending the sounds in words – word reading

- Check that the text makes sense as you read and correct inaccurate reading – comprehension

- Predict what might happen on the basis of what has been read so far – comprehension

- Read words containing common suffixes – word reading

- Read accurately recognising alternative sounds for graphemes – word reading

References

Bald, J (2007) *Using Phonics to Teach Reading and Spelling*. London: Paul Chapman Publishing.

Brooks, G (2003) *Sound Sense: The Phonics Element of the NLS: A Report to the DfES*. London: DfES.

Bullock Report (1975) *A Language for Life*. London: Her Majesty's Stationery Office.

Davis, A (2013) To read or not to read: Decoding synthetic phonics. *Impact: Philosophical Perspectives on Education Policy*, 20: 1–38.

Department for Education (DfE) (2012) *Research Evidence on Reading for Pleasure*. London: DfE.

Department for Education (DfE) (2013) *The National Curriculum in England: Framework Document*. London: DfE.

Department for Education and Employment (DfEE) (1998) *The National Literacy Strategy Framework for Teaching*. London: DfEE.

Department for Education and Skills (DfES) (2006) *Primary National Strategy: Primary Framework for Literacy and Mathematics*. London: DfES.

Ellis, S and Moss, G (2014) Ethics, education policy and research: The phonics question reconsidered. *British Educational Research Journal*, 40 (2): 241–60.

Farmer, S, Ellis, S and Smith, V (2006) Teaching phonics: The basics, in Lewis, M and Ellis, S (eds.) *Phonics, Practice, Research and Policy*. London: SAGE, pp35–45.

Gaiman, N (2014) *Reading and Obligation*. Speech to the Reading Agency [online]. Available at: **http://readingagency.org.uk/news/blog/neil-gaiman-lecture-in-full.html** [accessed 8 December 2014].

Goodman, K (1967) A psycholinguistic guessing game. *Journal of the Reading Specialist*, 6: 126–35.

Goswami, U (2010) Phonology, reading and reading difficulties, in Hall, K, Goswami, U, Harrison, C, Ellis, S and Soler, J (eds.) *Interdisciplinary Perspectives on Learning to Read*. London: Routledge, pp103–16.

Gough, PB and Tunmer, WE (1986) Decoding, reading and reading disability. *Remedial and Special Education*, 7: 6–10.

Hall, K, Goswami, U, Harrison, C, Ellis, S and Soler, J (eds.) (2010) *Interdisciplinary Perspectives on Learning to Read*. London: Routledge.

Huey, EG (1968) *The Psychology and Pedagogy of Reading*. Cambridge, MA: MIT Press (original work published 1908).

Johnston, R and Watson, J (2005) *The Effects of Synthetic Phonics Teaching of Reading and Spelling Attainment: A Seven-Year Longitudinal Study* [online]. Available at: **www.scotland.gov.uk/Resource/Doc/36496/0023582.pdf** [accessed 2 January 2015].

Jolliffe, W and Waugh, D with Carss, A (2012) *Teaching Systematic Synthetic Phonics in Primary Schools*. London: SAGE/Learning Matters.

Kirby, JR and Savage, R (2008) Can the simple view deal with complexities of reading? *Literacy*, 42 (2): 75–82.

Lewis, M and Ellis, S (eds.) (2006) *Phonics, Practice, Research and Policy*. London: SAGE.

Mora, JK (2001) Learning to spell in two languages: Orthographic transfer in a transitional Spanish/English bilingual program, in P Dreyer (ed.) *Raising Scores, Raising Questions: Claremont Reading Conference 65th Yearbook*. Claremont, CA: Claremont Graduate University, pp64–84.

Organisation for Economic Co-operation and Development (OECD) (2002) *Reading for Change: Performance and Engagement across Countries*. Results from PISA 2000. New York: OECD.

Plowden Report (1967) *Children and Their Primary Schools: A Report of the Central Advisory Council for Education (England)*. London: Her Majesty's Stationery Office.

Rose, J (2006) *The Independent Review of the Teaching of Early Reading*. London: Department for Children, Schools and Families (DCSF).

Stuart, M, Stainthorp, R and Snowling, M (2008) Literacy as a complex activity: Deconstructing the simple view of reading. *Literacy*, 42 (2): 59–66.

Washtell, A (2010) Getting to grips with phonics, in Graham, J and Kelly, A (eds.) *Reading under Control: Teaching Reading in the Primary School*. London: Routledge.

Wyse, D and Styles, M (2007) Synthetic phonics and the teaching of reading: The debate surrounding England's 'Rose Report'. *Literacy*, 41 (1): 35–42.

Chapter 2

Phonics in context

Learning outcomes

This chapter will allow you to achieve the following outcomes:

- develop an understanding of the role of the four strands of language in the teaching of reading and phonics in particular;
- gain a knowledge of approaches to creating a rich literate environment;
- develop an understanding of what is meant by the application of phonics across the curriculum.

Teachers' Standards

Working through this chapter will help you meet the following standards:

3. Demonstrate good subject and curriculum knowledge:

- Have a secure knowledge of the relevant subject(s) and curriculum areas, foster and maintain pupils' interest in the subject, and address misunderstandings.
- Demonstrate a critical understanding of developments in the subject and curriculum areas, and promote the value of scholarship.
- Demonstrate an understanding of and take responsibility for promoting high standards of literacy, articulacy and the correct use of standard English, whatever the teacher's specialist subject.
- If teaching early reading, demonstrate a clear understanding of systematic synthetic phonics.

Introduction

One of the key messages of the *Independent Review of the Teaching of Early Reading* (Rose, 2006, p16) was that phonic work should *be securely embedded within a broad and language rich curriculum* that *fosters all four interdependent strands of language: speaking, listening, reading and writing.* How to achieve this is the focus of the chapter.

Much of the research outlined in the previous chapter seems to highlight differences in approaches to phonics teaching; however, one thing that the research does agree on is that phonics is one element of the teaching of reading as part of a rich literacy curriculum (Ehri *et al.*, 2001) and that phonics 'should be part of every literacy teacher's repertoire and a routine part of literacy teaching, in a judicious balance with other elements' (Torgerson *et al.*, 2006, p49). The ultimate aim of the teaching and learning of phonics is for children to develop as independent readers who are motivated and engaged. This requires the teacher to ensure that:

- phonics teaching is lively, creative, focused and engaging;
- children learn within an environment that encourages children to talk about reading and engage and respond to text;
- the physical learning environment encourages children to apply their learning by using displays and prompts and also facilitates children's engagement and enjoyment of text;
- the application of phonics skills is planned, deliberately taught and modelled in reading and writing;
- children have regular incidental opportunities to apply their phonic learning to reading and writing within a learning environment that invites children to use their knowledge and skills.

Children need to see themselves as readers and writers from the start of their learning and be encouraged to read and write independently at every opportunity. When phonics is first introduced, it can initially make children feel nervous; suddenly there is a realisation that there is what they perceive as a right and wrong way to read and spell (Bower, 2011). The classroom ethos therefore needs to encourage children to use their emerging skills and knowledge confidently. Children need to feel they are real readers and writers and to be secure in the knowledge that all readers and writers make mistakes and use these mistakes to learn and improve.

In fact, very early on in a phonics programme (by the end of Phase 3 of Letters and Sounds) (DfES, 2007) children have one way to spell each of the 44 phonemes and so are able to write any word they want to. This may mean that they spell 'teddy' as 'tedee' and 'bear' as 'bair', but these attempts are phonically plausible and demonstrate the application of phonics learning to spelling – and this application is one of the keys to future success.

The literate environment: The language-rich curriculum

The literate environment is a rather catch-all term that describes:

- the physical classroom environment including displays and resources;
- the physical organisation of the learning environment that facilitates language development;

- teaching based on secure subject knowledge of children's literature and an understanding of how to use literature to enthuse, engage and deepen understanding of text;

- the planned role of talk in learning.

Together, all of these aspects create a classroom that is language-rich.

The physical environment: Displays and resources

A quick glance around a classroom gives the observer a good idea of how reading in particular, but writing as well, is valued by the teacher and school. Below are some ideas for resources and displays that create a rich language environment.

Displays of children's writing

Valuing children's writing from the earliest stage and making this value evident in the classroom is one essential ingredient of the language-rich classroom. These sorts of displays are often linked to topic-based displays that contain key vocabulary. Whatever the topic or classroom focus for a week or term, the language and key vocabulary of the topic needs to be made visible for children. It is really helpful to have this vocabulary on hook-and-loop fastener backed cards, so that words can be taken from the display to the child's writing area or taken by the teacher and studied together as a class, looking closely at how the word is spelled and how it is read. It is the interactive nature of the display that makes it useful and avoids a display becoming the backdrop to learning rather than an integral part of the learning.

The phonics grapheme chart or wall display

Most phonics schemes have matched resources including wall displays that consolidate the particular 'hooks' of the programme. The 'hook' refers to the way that the scheme supports children's memory of the grapheme–phoneme correspondences (GPC). For example, the Jolly Phonics scheme has wall charts with the rhyme, picture and song associated with each grapheme; so 'a' has a picture of an ant and a picture of a girl making the action of ants running up her arm. In the Read Write Inc. programme (Miskin, 2011) the grapheme is accompanied by a short phrase and picture, so the 'ay' grapheme has a picture of children playing and the phrase, 'May I play'. For a child, the introduction of graphemes is much like introducing mysterious black squiggles on a page and so the 'hook' gives children another anchor for remembering each GPC – often children will forget the sound the grapheme makes, but on recognising the 'hook', the picture or rhyme they are reminded of the associated sound.

It is important to be aware that it is not just about having the charts available, but about the deliberate teaching of how to use these charts when stuck in reading or writing. When modelling reading, it is sometimes a good idea to model what to do when you get stuck on a word and in this modelling process to wonder out loud how you will 'work it out'. Refer to the wall chart to show what you do when you can't remember a particular grapheme. Using puppets or special toys – for this often captures the imagination of younger children – the puppet struggles to read a word (or spell a word) and the teacher can help the puppet by taking him/her to the wall display and showing the puppet how to use the phoneme chart to help. The aim is for children to use the environmental displays independently as they are reading and writing.

Best guess displays

In Key Stage 1 and Key Stage 2 children are learning the alternative graphemes for each sound (Phase 5 of Letters and Sounds) (DfES, 2007). For example, if I want to spell a word with the 'ay' sound in it, I need to know the possible options for spelling it: ay; ai; a-e; eigh; a; and the list goes on. Having the choices made visible is a first step in selecting the correct choice, and so a readily accessible complex grapheme chart that displays the common representations of each sound is very useful to have in the classroom, both on the wall and on tables.

However, some choices are more common than others and some choices can be determined by the position of the sound in the word. For example, the 'best guesses' for spelling the 'ay' sound at the end of a word is 'a-e' or 'ay' rather than 'ai', which is more likely to be found if heard in the middle of the word. The Centre for Literacy in Primary Education (CLPE) suggests including wall displays that make these 'best guesses' visible, for example a display of fish of different sizes, the biggest fish with the most common spelling of the grapheme and a slightly smaller fish with the second most common spelling and so on. Each fish also has some additional helpful information about where in the word it is most commonly found. Details of the 'best guesses' can be found in the 'rules and guidance' section of the Spelling appendices in the National Curriculum (DfE, 2013, pp50–72).

Again, as with the phonics chart displays, children need to be directed to use these independently. During shared writing, part of the modelling of writing needs to include the teacher showing how to use the 'best guess' display; wondering out loud the thought processes of spelling a word and choice making where there is more than one possible grapheme for the sound needed.

Role play areas

These provide rich language contexts for reading and writing. The role play area should be 'drenched' in language, including key vocabulary, captions and labels.

They offer children real audiences and purposes for reading and writing. Watch the clip of children in the role play area which is set up as a travel agent's, at **https://www.youtube.com/watch?v=yt69atPdg3I**.

This shows how the children draw on and apply their knowledge of phonics, reading and writing, as well as their real life experiences of a travel agent. It is important to note that, just like the other examples in this section, the children's interactions haven't happened by accident; they happen because of careful planning by the teacher. It is likely that children have been taken to a real travel agent; they will have had time to talk about this experience with the teacher highlighting and recording key vocabulary; the teacher will have modelled how to behave in the role play area, e.g. by demonstrating to the children how to flick through a box file scanning the contents until the right card is found; by modelling how to record details of a proposed trip using the pro-forma prepared, including modelling the process of thinking aloud about grapheme–phoneme correspondences needed to complete the form. All of this teaching will have happened within the context of play, with the teacher 'playing' alongside the children.

The book corner

A language-rich classroom should have children's literature in all its forms at its heart. The OFSTED report *Excellence in English* (2011, p2) noted that *Schools that take the business of reading for pleasure seriously, where teachers read, talk with enthusiasm and recommend books, and where provision for reading is planned carefully, are more likely to succeed with their pupils' reading.* Gambrell (1996, p20) identified some key factors in developing reading: a *teacher who is a reading model; access to a book rich classroom environment; being able to choose books oneself; being familiar with books; social interactions with others about books; incentives that reflect the value of reading.* The book corner needs to be the hub of the activity that OFSTED and Gambrell identify.

Clearly, the book corner needs to be stocked with books that are of interest to children, and so it is important to both know your children and know children's books. Cremin *et al.* (2008) identified that teachers' knowledge of children's literature tended to be quite narrow and that they relied on books they had read as children to use in the classroom. While keeping up to date with children's literature and reading can be time consuming alongside planning, marking and assessment, it needs to be viewed as integral to teachers' subject knowledge of the teaching of reading. This knowledge is part of the planning process. One way to keep on top of the volume of wonderful children's literature is to keep an eye on children's book award pages. The UK Literacy Association (UKLA) children's book award is a good starting point (see **www.ukla.org/awards**).

One of the criteria for this award is *writing which offers language rich in layered meanings, imaginative expression and exciting vocabulary. Where present, high quality illustration is also an important feature of the chosen texts.*

The book corner offers ways for children to apply their phonic learning in context, both in terms of reading and writing. Consider encouraging writing in the book corner using the following ideas:

- a message board where children can write about their favourite book;

- sticky notes available that children can write on and then stick on their favourite page of a book with a message for the reader who finds it;

- strips of card that can be put around a book with readers' views, or book jackets made by the children. Hardback books often come with a book jacket, but these can be made for paperback books too, and enable children to decide what they would put on the front cover, the blurb at the back, and their reviewer comments;

- posters sharing the author of the week;

- pieces of card available for children to note down their favourite words or phrases;

- a reading tree, with leaves available to stick to the tree with recommendations and pictures of favourite parts.

The book corner also needs to include all sorts of other authentic texts: leaflets; cinema guides; maps; recipes; magazines; newspapers; school newsletters as well as electronic texts.

Games and activities in and outside the classroom

There are lots of published games, but games can be made and adapted to match the context of topics or role play areas. Children in the early years (or Key Stage 1 and 2) can be encouraged to access these independently or they can be used to support teaching and assessment if a teaching assistant, adult volunteer or the teacher leads them. Try the following ideas.

Fishing

Make a number of fishing rods with paper clip hooks on the end. In a bucket or sugar paper pond, put a number of paper fish with small magnets attached. Each fish has a decodable word on it. Children 'fish' for the fish and keep their fish if they are able to sound and blend the word. Play the game a number of times, moving children from sounding and blending to automatic decoding, i.e. able to read the word without needing to sound and blend.

Shops

Provide children with lots of objects to sell in a shop. Tell the children the shop labels with their prices have become detached and their job is to match the label to the object. This works well when setting up a shop role play area.

Twister

Create a *Twister* mat (originally produced by Hasbro), a mat divided into a number of squares. Rather than colours, each square has a word written in it. Have a replica small board and a die. Roll the die and whichever word it lands on is where the first child puts his or her left foot – the child has to read and confirm the word before standing on it. The die is rolled again and this indicates where the right foot should be placed and so on.

Outdoor recipes

Write a list of outdoor ingredients children need to collect to create a special potion. This might include: 3 sticks; 2 scoops of mud; 1 leaf; 1 snail; 3 ants. Link this idea to stories like *George's Marvellous Medicine* by Roald Dahl to give it a real context. Ensure that the words selected are phonically decodable at the phonic phase the participants are learning.

Many of these games and more can be found at **www.pininterest.com**.

Search for phonics games. Most of these are things you can make yourself, especially if you filter the games using the DIY tab.

Planned opportunities for application: Reading

Every discrete phonics lesson should include opportunities for children to apply their new learning to reading and writing. This may take the form of reading the newly taught grapheme–phoneme correspondence (GPC) on a series of flash cards (common in schemes such as Read Write Inc.) or reading a caption or short sentence or the application in a game or activity. This is an essential part of phonics teaching, but the application needs to go beyond the phonics lesson. Guthrie (2008), when discussing motivation and choice in reading and writing, talks about 'teaching that travels'. This means teaching that is echoed from discrete teaching to and across other parts of the day and curriculum.

OFSTED's (2010, p28) *Reading by Six: How the Best Schools Do It* states that *the best teachers made frequent recourse to phonic decoding strategies when the class encountered unfamiliar words in other areas of the curriculum.* This means that whenever reading is used across the school day (to read instructions; to find out about an element of the topic; when using the computer; making choices from the lunch menu), reading is taught. These opportunities become deliberate acts of teaching and deliberate prompts for children to apply their phonics skills and knowledge independently.

This further supports children's memory of the GPCs. In the early stages, children have to master the GPCs so that they become automatic and subconscious. Repetition, review and revisiting in different contexts support this process. The physical environment and its incidental learning opportunities are one route to reaching automaticity, but planned opportunities to apply in reading and writing are also needed. Some key ways to do this are outlined in the next section.

Phonically decodable text

The National Curriculum (2013, p20) states that children in Year 1 should *Read aloud accurately books that are consistent with their developing phonics knowledge and that do not require them to use other strategies to work out the words.* This is consistent with the earlier guidance set out in the Department for Education's Core Criteria (2010, p2), which outlines the key features that are required when schools are considering which phonics programme to purchase, when auditing phonics provision in a school, or creating a school phonics scheme of work. One of these criteria states that a phonics programme must *ensure that as pupils move through the early stages of acquiring phonics, they are invited to practise by reading texts which are entirely decodable for them, so that they experience success and learn to rely on phonemic strategies.* A phonically decodable text is a graded text with a vocabulary controlled in relation to the phonemes it uses. Snow *et al.* (1998) maintained that decodable texts provided opportunities for children in the early stages of learning to read to apply their decoding skills in context.

The key to each of these statements concerns the clarity of purpose for their use as a strategy in the teaching of early reading. That is to say, the texts' purpose is to give children the opportunity to apply their phonic learning at a level at which they will have success in reading. The decodable text, because of its controlled and thus limited vocabulary, is rarely a language-rich feast. It does not often have an exciting or engaging plot with interesting characters and settings, but it must be remembered that this is not its prime purpose. It is designed for the teaching and application of newly learnt phonics skills and knowledge. However, even though this is the main purpose, it is still important to remember that these are often the first texts that children will encounter as independent readers and so must be presented to children in a way that will engage and motivate them as readers.

Ideas for applying phonics in the context of the decodable text: Engaging and motivating

Before reading:

- Start by looking together at the front cover and predict what the story might be about; wonder who the main characters are, what they are doing and why; make links to children's prior knowledge about similar situations and texts.

- 'Walk' through the book, looking at the pictures and discussing what the story might be about. Teach any unusual vocabulary – this is particularly important with the decodable text, as the author will have been working with a limited set of phonemes and therefore some word choices can be a little unusual or unfamiliar to the child. For example, in a Phase 3 Bug Club book is the sentence 'A shark is lurking'. The word 'lurking' may need to be discussed and explained. What you need to guard against with the decodable text is a child decoding fluently and effortlessly, but not understanding the story they have read because they are not comprehending the individual words. This text walk-through is also useful to revisit newly introduced GPCs and tricky words (see Chapter 11). This process builds confidence and also ensures the balance needed between decoding and comprehension.

During and after reading:

- Read the book, but return for a re-reading two or three times. Each revisit enables the child to develop automaticity in reading, and each revisit can have a different focus. For example, on the second reading you may pause more frequently to ask questions; to discuss thoughts and feelings about the story and characters; to act out some of the scenes; and so focus more closely on comprehension, response and engagement. A third reading may focus on noticing the punctuation and so developing fluency and expression.

- If you return to a text a number of times, it is useful to make it clear to parents the different purposes of each of your readings and, in particular, parents need to understand the need to balance decoding and comprehension. Time spent at home talking about the book before, during and after reading is as valuable as the reading itself.

It is, however, useful to note that for several decades researchers have commented on the limitations of reading schemes (and not just those with a vocabulary controlled in relation to phonics) in motivating and inducting children into the world of a reader (Beard, 1990; Browne, 2009; Meek, 1991). The limitations of schemes with regard to developing positive attitudes to reading were also noted by Her Majesty's Inspectorate (HMI) in England in their report *Reading for Purpose and Pleasure* (OFSTED, 2004).

With this in mind, it is important to balance the use of the decodable text with other high-quality children's literature, and this is what is meant by a 'broad and balanced' literacy curriculum. Developing the book corner, as outlined above, ensuring there is time through the day to read aloud to children, and planning shared and guided reading using high-quality literature, all ensure that the reading curriculum is both broad and balanced.

Shared and guided reading

Shared reading is a whole-class activity. It involves sharing one text, which could be an enlarged text, a big book, or more commonly, a text shared using the interactive white board, either in the form of extracts from a longer text that has been read to the class or an ebook. Shared reading enables children to have access to texts that are above their current reading attainment levels and so engage in collaborative comprehension activities in response to and engaging with the text (Goodwin, 2011).

However, shared reading also offers the opportunity to apply phonics skills and knowledge within the context of reading. Shared reading enables teachers to model how they tackle unknown words – modelling how to sound and blend. It is helpful to consider the sorts of difficulties your class has with decoding and use these as the basis for teaching. Many children make good progress initially with blending to read within Phase 2, but when introduced to more consonant and vowel digraphs they can find it more difficult to recognise these as a unit within a word, and so sound each individual letter.

This can be the basis of focused teaching in shared reading, modelling the error and then thinking aloud that this word doesn't make sense or doesn't sound like a real word. The teacher can model having a closer look at the word, spotting on the second reading the digraph and then re-blending the word. It is important to model the re-reading of the sentence to check the newly decoded word now makes sense.

Another common issue for children as they start to learn to read is that they use their phonics skills of sounding and blending even when they do not need to, i.e. when they encounter a word they know, rather than reading the whole word they sound and blend it anyway. It may be a word that they have encountered many times before and yet they don't yet have the confidence to say the whole word – automatically decoding (Pressley, 2002). Teachers can use shared reading to model how to use sounding and blending for words they are not sure how to read, and also reading whole words where the decoding is automatic. The teacher can model the re-reading of sentences, checking that what they have read makes sense and so keeping the purpose of reading for meaning as a constant focus.

Guided reading gives teachers the opportunity to work with a smaller group of children who are reading at about the same reading attainment level. Each child in the group has a copy of the text. In the early stages of reading, this smaller group allows the teacher to really match the learning objectives to the precise needs of the group. The teacher is able to begin the session with a revision of phonemes that children are finding particularly difficult. This could be in the form of a short game or direct teaching. The children then move on to reading the text. The process outlined above for using a decodable text can apply in a guided reading session, as can the approaches outlined as part of shared reading.

Planned opportunities for application: Writing

Developing children's confidence as writers is the key to developing children's application of their phonic skills and knowledge. Shared writing is the opportunity to teach the application of skills in the context of the writing process. In the same way as described for shared reading, shared writing allows the teacher to demonstrate the thought processes of a writer, including the process of oral rehearsal (saying the sentence to be written out loud) and the process of spelling each word. We do not often consider how we go about spelling a word as an adult, but the process needs to be carefully broken down and modelled for the child.

The following six steps are helpful to follow.

1. Say the word out loud, articulating the word clearly.

2. Say the word again, but the second time segmenting the word into its constituent phonemes, holding up a finger for each phoneme that is segmented.

3. Say the word again, pressing the sounds identified onto each finger, deliberately emphasising the sounds.

4. Write the word, carefully articulating each grapheme needed for each sound.

5. Re-read what has been written to check that it says the word that was intended.

6. Re-read the sentence to check the sentence says what was intended, before moving on to the next word to spell.

When using shared writing you need to get a flow going for the writing, so it is useful to only model the spelling/segmenting process for a few chosen words in the writing.

Shared writing should model writing for different purposes and for different audiences and needs to be followed by children having an opportunity to apply their skills independently. Marsh and Hallet (2008) provide a really useful list of different types of real writing contexts that children can engage with independently. These include *coupons and forms; envelopes; postcards and greeting cards representing a variety of festivals and featuring a range of languages; note and message pads; in- and out-trays; diaries and calendars*.

Conclusion

When teaching phonics it is essential to keep in mind the purpose of teaching phonics: to teach children to read and write. Phonics knowledge on its own, or even the decoding and encoding of single words, are not reading and writing in their true sense. Reading and writing are purposeful, real life activities and so the deliberate application of phonics teaching embedded in these different contexts for different audiences and purposes is an essential part of successful teaching.

Learning outcomes review

You should now understand the role of the four strands of language (speaking, listening, reading and writing) in the teaching of reading and phonics. You should be aware of approaches to creating a rich literate environment and understand what is meant by the application of phonics across the curriculum.

References

Beard, R (1990) *Developing Reading 3–13*. London: Hodder and Stoughton.

Bower, V (2011) *Creative Ways to Teach Literacy*. London: SAGE.

Browne, A (2009) *Developing Language and Literacy 3–8*. London: SAGE.

Cremin, T, Mottram, M, Bearne, E and Goodwin, P (2008) Exploring teachers' knowledge of children's literature. *Cambridge Journal of Education*, 38 (4): 449–64.

Department for Education (DfE) (2010) *Phonics Teaching Materials: Core Criteria and Self-Assessment*. Available at: **www.gov.uk/government/publications/phonics-teaching-materials-core-criteria-and-self-assessment** [accessed 18 May 2015].

Department for Education (DfE) (2013) *The National Curriculum in England: Framework Document*. London: DfE. Available at: **www.gov.uk/dfe/nationalcurriculum** [accessed 18 May 2015].

Department for Education and Skills (DfES) (2007) *Letters and Sounds: Principles and Practice of High Quality Phonics*. London: DfES.

Ehri, L, Nunes, SR, Stahl, SA and Willows, DM (2001) Systematic phonics instruction helps students learn to read: Evidence from the National Reading Panel's meta-analysis. *Review of Education*, 71 (3): 393–447.

Gambrell, LB (1996) Creating classroom cultures that foster reading motivation. *The Reading Teacher*, 50: 14–25.

Goodwin, P (2011) *The Literate Classroom* (3rd edn.). London: David Fulton.

Guthrie, JT (ed.) (2008) *Engaging Adolescents in Reading*. Thousand Oaks, CA: Corwin Press.

Marsh, J and Hallet, E (2008) *Desirable Literacies: Approaches to Language and Literacies in the Early Years*. London: SAGE.

Meek, M (1991) *On Becoming Literate*. London: Bodley Head.

Miskin, R (2011) *Read Write Inc.: Phonics Handbook*. Oxford: Oxford University Press.

OFSTED (2004) *Reading for Purpose and Pleasure: An Evaluation of the Teaching of Reading in Primary Schools*. London: OFSTED.

OFSTED (2010) *Reading by Six: How the Best Schools Do It*. London: Paul Chapman.

OFSTED (2011) *Excellence in English: What We Can Learn from 12 Outstanding Schools*. May 2011, No. 100229. London: DfE.

Pressley, M (2002) Comprehension strategies instruction: A turn-of-the-century status report, in Block, CC and Pressley, M (eds.) *Comprehension Instruction: Research-Based Best Practices*. New York: Guilford, pp11–27.

Rose, J (2006) *The Independent Review of the Teaching of Early Reading*. London: Department for Children, Schools and Families (DCSF).

Snow, CE, Burns, MS and Griffin, P (1998) *Preventing Reading Difficulties in Young Children*. Washington, DC: National Academy Press.

Torgerson, CJ, Brooks, G and Hall, J (2006) *A Systematic Review of the Research Literature on the Use of Phonics in the Teaching of Reading and Spelling*. London: Department for Education and Skills (DfES).

Chapter 3

Reception: Developing phonemic awareness

Learning outcomes

This chapter will allow you to achieve the following outcomes:

- identify strategies to support teaching young children phonemes;
- recognise how we can support children to meet their Early Learning Goals at the end of Reception;
- be aware of some useful ICT resources for teaching and learning phonics;
- identify potential barriers to learning and reflect upon ways to overcome these.

Teachers' Standards

Working through this chapter will help you meet the following standards:

2. Promote good progress and outcomes by pupils:

- Be aware of pupils' capabilities and their prior knowledge, and plan teaching to build on these.

3. Demonstrate good subject and curriculum knowledge:

- Demonstrate an understanding of and take responsibility for promoting high standards of literacy, articulacy and the correct use of standard English, whatever the teacher's specialist subject.
- If teaching early reading, demonstrate a clear understanding of systematic synthetic phonics.

Links to the National Curriculum

Early Learning Goals (ELGs)

READING
Children use phonic knowledge to decode regular words and read them aloud accurately. They also read some common irregular words.

WRITING

Children use their phonic knowledge to write words in ways which match their spoken sounds. They also write some irregular common words. They write simple sentences which can be read by themselves and others. Some words are spelt correctly and others are phonetically plausible.

(DfE, 2013, pp21–2)

How do children learn to use phonemes?

A phoneme is the smallest unit of sound in speech. When we teach reading we teach children which letters represent those sounds. This is most effective when children can explore using play, hearing songs and rhymes, and playing with letters.

Before children develop awareness of phonemes, they need to develop their 'phonological awareness'. Phonological awareness is the ability to perceive, recall and manipulate sounds. This can be done in a variety of ways, including exploring sounds in the environment, listening to and discriminating between sounds made by musical instruments, listening to and joining in with songs, stories and poems, and playing word games orally. The aim of all of these activities is to develop children's listening skills to enable them to discriminate between sounds, remember sounds and sequences of sounds and talk about sounds. All of this will help children when they come to learn to hear and discriminate between phonemes.

'Phonemic awareness' involves understanding that letters can be sounded as phonemes and can be put together to create words. This should, initially, be developed orally through games and activities such as:

Teacher: I'm thinking of someone's name. It begins with /n/.

[Teacher enunciates *nnn*]. Could it be Sarah? Could it be Rachel? Could it be Nick?

Children are asked to answer and then take turns to do the same thing for other names in the class.

Children come to school with levels of different phonemic awareness. Some may have a strong understanding of and ability to apply knowledge of how phonemes function in words, while others may have little to no phonemic awareness. It is essential that an Early Years practitioner creates a language-rich curriculum. This could include a print-rich classroom, phonics resources, big books, magnetic letters, use of ICT and an inviting reading area. By surrounding children with texts, they see the importance of words and reading and regard it as a natural part of everyday life. This can range from having children's names on drawers and in the cloakroom, to having dates on the board and lists of things to do, to having displays of poems, stories, words beginning with certain letters, maps and comics.

Teaching your class: Supporting oral and aural phonemic awareness

Alliteration

Children enjoy phrases and jingles with repetitive sounds. Start by using their names and asking them to think of alliterative adjectives to go with them (you might not use the term 'adjective' at this stage, although children in Year 2 will learn it). You could have: *Funny Farouk, Happy Harry, Nice Nick, Super Sarah, Lucky Lucy* and *Smiley Seima.* Go on to make alliterative phrases for things children can see around the classroom. You could take them for a walk around the school to look for more examples.

Sound bags

Collect objects and pictures that have names/words beginning with the same sound. In preparation for looking at early letters (*s,a,t,p,i,n*) you might have a bag for each letter. Ask children to take items from a bag and to name them. Model how you can emphasise the initial sound so that you say *s-s-s-sock* and *s-s-s-satsuma* and then ensure that children have a go at doing the same. Begin by using two bags and go on to use more as children's phonemic awareness develops. Once all the items are out of both bags, ask children to sort them out and put them into the correct bags. Label the bags with the appropriate letters, as this will help you to lead into graphemic representations of the sounds.

Oral word building

Choose some of the items from your bags that have up to three phonemes and sound them slowly, for example: *sss-o-ck, p-a-n*. After saying the sounds always say the word, so after sounding *sss-o-ck* say the word *sock*. This enables the child to identify the sounds in words, but also to orally blend them together to make the word. Ask children to sound them after you and, when they are ready, ask them to sound them without your help.

Using bead strings for blending

Use a range of short words and names and sound these slowly for the children, then with them and finally let them sound them without your help. Give children simple strings of beads and ask them to move a bead for each sound they can hear/identify. This supports children in identifying how many sounds are within a word.

Throwing a ball for each sound

To ensure that children can hear sounds within a word, ask them to throw/bounce a ball for each sound they can hear. You could incorporate this activity into PE lessons or you could take the children to the playground. They could also clap or tap on a table.

Commentary

It is important that children learn to hear all the phonemes in a word if they are to be able to read and then write accurately. However, many adults, having long passed the stage where they analyse words in this way, are not explicitly aware of individual phonemes in words. Instead, when looking at familiar words attention is drawn to the meaning and letters tend to be clustered together into familiar patterns (str-, -tion, -ing, etc.). A common misconception in trainee teachers can be illustrated by looking at a word like stitch. *Because we are used to seeing consonant clusters like* st *at the beginning of words, we might think that* st *is a single phoneme, when in fact it is a blend of two phonemes:* s *and* t *(try saying* st *and notice that your tongue moves as you make each sound. In fact,* stitch *has four phonemes: /s/t/i/tch/, with* tch *being a trigraph – three letters making one phoneme.*

Activity: Segmenting

Look at the following words and segment them into individual phonemes. Remember that you tend to make different movements in your mouth each time you sound a different phoneme.

black   ditch   swish   stump

Developing children's ability to relate phonemes to graphemes

Flash cards using gestures, e.g. Jolly Phonics/ Read Write Inc. (Miskin, 2011)

Many programmes use gestures or actions to reinforce the sounds children are learning. Make cards that show letters and an item or animal which is familiar to children for each one. You might have *ant, banana, cat, dog*, etc. As they look at the cards and say the sounds they can make appropriate mimed gestures. In Jolly Phonics, for example, *s* has a snake and children make a *ssss* sound, while for *t* there is a picture of a game of tennis and they make a *t* sound while turning their heads from side to side as if watching a match.

Marble run letters

Children identify sounds in their name/sound being taught that day/week. As they move the marble around the letter they say the sound it makes, and the phrase or action that may go with the sound. This will reinforce the sound and also enable them to understand how to write the sound.

Using phoneme frames

Look at simple, phonically regular words that children often use, for example: *cat, dog, mat, sit, sat, pin, pat, sun*. After saying the word ask children to identify the first and second sounds (or phonemes) in the word. This activity helps children realise that words are made up of a series of independent sounds or phonemes. It will be helpful to support children when beginning to blend. Work on all three sounds on the words and use phoneme frames to separate the graphemes that represent each phoneme.

Body gym

Play simple games like Simon Says, but after initially saying things like *Simon says touch your nose*, go on to use only the initial sound of the thing to be touched or done: *Simon says touch your nnn ..., Simon says put your hands on your sh ...,* etc. Go on to sound all of the sounds in the word: *Simon says touch your l-e-g.* Children will need to blend the sounds orally to identify which body part to touch. Because this is oral blending, any word can be sounded for children.

You can develop this at different times of the day, for example when children are lining up to go to assembly or coming in from the playground and you want to settle them down in a purposeful way. Get children to take over from you to say what Simon says, once they are confident.

Key focus: Developing phonemic awareness

Children develop an awareness of print from a very early age. They identify logos, signs, text and learn to associate these with meaning. Try showing them words and symbols for well-known cars, shops and restaurants to see what they know already. Their awareness of print expands as they assign meaning to sounds. Those who are exposed to print in a language-rich environment are likely to become good readers. Children who are able to identify sounds/words in newspapers, cookery books and signs often become curious and engaged with the subject. As a teacher, you need to look for opportunities to expose children to print and create this environment inside school.

Some ideas for this include the following.

- Shared reading: ensures that children are sharing stories as an adult-led activity, including questioning them, encouraging them to join in and make predictions.

- Guided reading: teaches the principles of reading. It supports children in identifying the author and illustrator, in learning that print has meaning and that we read from left to right. Guided reading is important for teaching children how to read in a supported capacity. It also provides the opportunity for extended talk about text.

- Story sacks: enable children to tell stories with props or re-enact the story. It allows children to be creative and engages them using their storyteller voice. This is often how children begin to use expression independently.

- Use of puppets: allows children to re-tell stories through the mask of another. Puppets can help shy children to express themselves.

- Story maps: allow children to re-tell stories, exploring their creative side. Pie Corbett has a range of stories with maps for teachers to use if you are not confident in creating your own maps to begin with. Children will, of course, often naturally create pictures from stories and mapping is just an extension of this. Further ideas can be found at **www.talk4writing.co.uk**.

- Hearing rhyme: rhyme is a great way to help your class develop their language and communication skills. Rhymes also help us to learn to play with words. They tune our ears to all the sounds in a word. By hearing different sounds we learn how sounds combine and blend together to form a word.

- Modelling writing: helps put meaning to print. Supporting children when modelling on the board helps children to identify how we write. This will encourage children to ask questions and begin to copy even if they cannot form letters. Early print is key for children's development. The more they grow in confidence, the more it will support them as they begin to blend and segment.

Teaching phonemic awareness

Exposure, practice and hearing the new sound

Enable children to hear the sound being taught. This could be done using pictures, objects or a children's dictionary. Children need to become familiar with the sound before learning to use it. Alongside hearing the sound, children should say the sound; this could be the sound on its own, using the sound within a word, or finding the sound (this could be done using flash cards of previously taught sounds or finding the sound within a word). When children become familiar with the sound and are actively participating, they are more likely to remember it.

Explore and investigate using the sound

Once children have heard the sound and said the sound, they can go on to investigate the sound. This could be done by selecting the sound using various pictures or objects. This will also help you to assess if they are able to hear the sound. Support children in assisted blending, and model how to blend, using simple consonant–vowel–consonant (CVC) words from letters you have previously taught. For example, in Letters and Sounds (DfES, 2007) the first sounds taught are *s,a,t,p,i,n*. Encourage children to repeat the sounds after you, ensuring they are saying the sounds correctly and not adding the *schwa* (in Read Write Inc. this is called using 'pure sounds').

Support children with assisted blending by using phoneme frames, objects to count the number of sounds or magnetic letters so children can identify the graphemes that match sounds they can hear. Support children during blending until they can do this independently.

Review, review, review!

All phonic programmes stress the importance of reviewing what children already know. Children learn through repetition. This could be at the beginning or the end of the lesson or at both the beginning and the end. Drip-feeding children phonics throughout the day can be an effective way of ensuring they are confident in hearing and saying the taught sounds. This could be using flash cards before the children go into assembly or reading CVC words in the playground hidden within the equipment and hanging from trees.

Main lesson

Teaching phonemes

This lesson is based upon the children having been taught *s,a,t,p,i,n*.

Practise the new sound

Show children the new sound. When introducing the new sound, try to think of a memorable way children can visualise the sound, e.g. Natalie is a nice nurse. Show them the written form of the sound *n*. Encourage the children to repeat the sound after you. Show the children examples of the sound being used within a word, e.g. *nest, night, nurse, net, nose, noodle*; this could be an actual object or a picture.

Explore and investigate

Show the children pictures, for example: *nurse, sad, pig, night, net*. Encourage them to choose pictures which have the /n/ sound within them. Ask them to say the words as they choose a picture. It is helpful if the other words are pictures including initial sounds that you have previously taught, as this will help support those who may not know their alphabet or may have limited vocabulary.

Give the children alphabet fans, say a sound the children know, and see if they can hold the right grapheme up. Those who are finding this difficult can work in pairs and will build confidence seeing others holding up their alphabet fan. Oral assisted blending is important here. Using the sounds the children know, blend a word, for example, *n-a-p – nap*. Say the sounds slowly again, asking the children to count how many sounds there are within the word. Ask the children questions such as: *What is the first sound? What is the second sound? What is the final sound?* Then ask the children to repeat the sounds after you, and keep repeating the sounds so that children can hear them, then ask them if they can hear what the word is. Once they can do this, write the word on a card and read it together, storing this card so that the children can continue to practise reading throughout the day. Repeat this with *pan, tan* and *ant,* etc.

Review

At this early stage, using the mnemonic you have taught is useful as some children will remember a picture or saying more easily than the sound. Review the sounds children have been taught, and then review the words the children had previously read. The more children are exposed to these and they are reviewed, the more likely they are to remember them. Finish the lesson by asking the children what sound they have learnt and revising the words they were able to blend.

Teaching phonemes to EAL children

Case study

Amir had a Spanish child, Rosa, in his class who couldn't speak any English. As the other children were already able to blend and were reading CVC words, Rosa seemed lost and confused. She often cried and wandered around the classroom. Amir looked at various websites including the BBC languages site and listened to and learned the Spanish alphabet and some simple vocabulary. He found he was able to model a lesson for Rosa using equivalent Spanish words so that she understood what the class would be doing. Even with very little English, she was able to identify the routine. This supported her throughout learning the English alphabet.

The main difficulty came when Rosa had to identify the pictures of objects (hearing/saying the sound). As she knew little English, she spoke the word in Spanish, which naturally had a different sound. For example, when learning the sound /a/, the class were saying *a-apple*, while Rosa identified it as *m-manzana*. Upon seeing the picture, she associated the word with the *m* sound. This presented a problem, so Amir continued, where possible, to identify words in Spanish as well as in English so that she could understand. As the routine went on, she relied on the class and Amir to give her the English word. Not only did this help to support Rosa's phonetic development, but it also enabled her to progress to learn English quickly. The rest of the class were also interested in the Spanish words Rosa knew and some were keen to learn bits of Spanish from her. This raised her self-esteem and meant that the children could see that she was bright and intelligent.

Use of ICT

ICT can be a powerful tool when teaching phonics. There are many games that children can use independently during Child Initiated Play, including the following.

- **www.bbc.co.uk/cbeebies/shows/alphablocks**. *Alphablocks* is a popular programme on BBC; their website provides games, television clips and printable sheets that children will enjoy. You can also buy story books with these characters which encourages children to use their phonic knowledge. The books also have prompts for adults in how to support their child.

- **www.mrthorne.com**. Mr Thorne Does Phonics has created his own brand using YouTube and mobile apps. These range from YouTube videos that are free to paid apps, which range in price.

- Jolly Phonics Letter Sounds by Jolly Learning. Available at: **http://jollylearning. co.uk**. In this app the characters discover the main 42 letter sounds of English through games.

- Teach Your Monster to Read: First Steps. Available at: **www. teachyourmonstertoread.com**. This app uses the teaching sequences of letters and sounds; it is a series of games that help children master the first stages of reading. It was designed in collaboration with leading academics from Roehampton University.

In this chapter you have seen the importance of teaching phonological and phonemic awareness in a lively, creative way in order to engage children's interest. As you look at subsequent chapters, bear in mind the value of interactive teaching and learning and consider the use of resources and visual aids to enhance your teaching.

Learning outcomes review

You should now be able to identify strategies to support teaching young children phonemes. You should also be able to identify some potential barriers to learning and reflect upon ways to overcome these.

Answers to segmenting activity (page 30)
You were asked to segment the following words into individual phonemes.

- black – /b/l/a/ck/ (4 phonemes)

- ditch – /d/i/tch/ (3 phonemes)

- swish – /s/w/i/sh/ (4 phonemes)

- stump – /s/t/u/m/p/ (5 phonemes)

If you struggled with this, try saying the segmented words slowly and think about the different movements in your mouth each time you sound a different phoneme.

Further reading

Jolliffe, W and Waugh, D with Carss, A (2015) *Teaching Systematic Synthetic Phonics in Primary Schools*. London: SAGE.

To develop your understanding of phonological and phonemic awareness, see Chapter 1 in particular.

The following websites provide helpful practical guidance on teaching phonics.

www.mrthorne.com/or – *Mr Thorne Does Phonics* [accessed 19 December 2014].

www.mrthorne.com – *Getting Reading* [accessed 19 December 2014].

References

BBC Languages Spanish (2015) Available at: **www.bbc.co.uk/languages/spanish/guide/alphabet.shtml** [accessed 6 April 2015].

Department for Education (DfE) (2013) *Early Years Outcomes*. A non-statutory guide for practitioners and inspectors to help inform understanding of child development through the early years. Available at: **www.gov.uk/government/publications** [accessed 6 April 2015].

Department for Education and Skills (DfES) (2007) *Letters and Sounds: Principles and Practice of High Quality Phonics*. London: DfES.

Miskin, R (2011) *Read Write Inc.: Phonics Handbook*. Oxford: Oxford University Press.

Chapter 4

Reception: Beginning to read and write using CVC words

Learning outcomes

This chapter will allow you to achieve the following outcomes:

- identify strategies to support teaching young children phonemes;
- recognise how we can support children to meet their Early Learning Goals at the end of Reception;
- be aware of possible uses of ICT when teaching phonics;
- identify potential barriers to learning and reflect upon ways to overcome these.

Teachers' Standards

Working through this chapter will help you meet the following standards:

3. Demonstrate good subject and curriculum knowledge:

- Demonstrate an understanding of and take responsibility for promoting high standards of literacy, articulacy and the correct use of standard English, whatever the teacher's specialist subject.
- If teaching early reading, demonstrate a clear understanding of systematic synthetic phonics.

4. Plan and teach well-structured lessons:

- Promote a love of learning and children's intellectual curiosity.

Links to the National Curriculum

Early Learning Goals (ELGs)

READING
Children use phonic knowledge to decode regular words and read them aloud accurately. They also read some common irregular words.

WRITING

Children use their phonic knowledge to write words in ways which match their spoken sounds. They also write some irregular common words. They write simple sentences which can be read by themselves and others. Some words are spelt correctly and others are phonetically plausible.

(DfE, 2013b, pp21–2)

Introduction

Many phonics programmes teach blending alongside teaching phonemes. Letters and Sounds (DfES, 2007) and Read Write Inc. (Miskin, 2011) teach blending after children know five sounds; with both programmes children start by blending using CVC (consonant–vowel–consonant) words. Both programmes stress the importance of repetition when blending.

What are CVC words?

CVC stands for 'consonant–vowel–consonant' and CVC words include *cat, dog, sit, pin*, etc. The early letter–sound correspondences taught in most phonic programmes (*s,a,t,p,i,n* or *m*) make it possible to create several CVC words; for example, *sat, mat, pat, pin, map, sin, sip, tip, tap, lap, pal*. For early reading teachers usually stick to CVC words of three letters. However, as children develop they can learn other CVC words which include consonant digraphs, such as *back, chip, shop, check*, and those that include vowel digraphs, such as *weep, bead, rain* and *shout*.

Activity: CVC words

Which of the following words are CVC words?

dock   shop   pig   day   boy   badge   watch   free   steep   help

Key focus: Teaching phonics and blending

Having a structure for teaching phonics is central to success. Children need to know what they are learning and why. It is also important to keep in mind the bigger picture of teaching, remembering that phonics is taught as an approach to teaching children to read and write. Keeping this in mind enables you to use the structure of a lesson to ensure progress within the lesson towards reading and writing – rather than the teaching and learning of phonemes as a goal in itself.

Having a structure that teachers follow enables children to have an expectation of what they will be learning. It encourages them to ask questions, notice patterns in what they are learning and become confident in what will come next. It also allows teachers to ensure that the pace of the lesson matches the needs of the class, enabling children to move seamlessly from one learning opportunity to another and to maintain motivation and interest through the lesson.

How children learn to blend

Children learn to blend through exploring using sounds and being supported through modelling. They need to hear the sounds being said seamlessly to be able to blend. You can begin by segmenting the sounds and breaking words up (*s-a-t*), but you should follow this by blending them together. The term 'synthetic phonics' stems from the idea that the sounds need to be synthesised or blended together in order to read words. It is vital that the teacher enunciates phonemes clearly and without a *schwa* ending. For many children blending is not an easy or natural process. Children who can hear the *onset* and *rime* in a word and are able to blend these larger chunks of sound are not able, necessarily, to do the same with smaller units of sound.

Commentary

*Some well-meaning parents and carers may already have taught children to sound letters with an extra vowel sound (*fuh *instead of* fff, luh *instead of* lll, suh *instead of* sss, *etc.). This can cause problems when blending sounds together and can lead to some odd spellings, such as 'bt' for 'butter' and 'cl' for 'colour', because children think that the vowel sound has been made by the consonant. Letters and Sounds (DfES, 2007) has a useful DVD which shows a mouth as you listen to phonemes being enunciated correctly. You could also look at the BBC's* Alphablocks *or at various weblinks to* Mr Thorne Does Phonics *to hear correct enunciation.*

Assisted blending

Assisted blending is the first stage of blending when children are first learning to blend sounds in a word to read. Assisted blending is a term used in the Read Write Inc. scheme and refers to the heavily scaffolded process of modelling to children how to blend sounds together. The teacher models the blending process with the graphemes most recently introduced. The children repeat or echo exactly what the teacher has demonstrated. Repetition is key in the early stages of reading. Read Write Inc. stresses the importance of 'my turn your turn' – a process in which the teacher models and the children copy, so that children can hear the sounds and hear how they become a word.

Assisted blending is taught as soon as children confidently know the first few sounds *s,a,t,p* (or *m,a,s,t,d* in Read Write Inc.) (when they can identify them and recall the sounds). Modelling blending for children is crucial at this stage of learning to read. White boards can be a useful resource to support this. On an interactive white board or using magnetic letters, the teacher can display the graphemes for the sounds children know. Having decided on a word the children are going to read, the teacher can pull down the sounds that are within the word, for example, *p-a-t*. The word can be displayed as a whole and at this stage the teacher is telling the children what the word they are going to read is.

Children can be encouraged to discuss how many sounds they can hear in the word. The teacher can read the word as a whole, then segmenting the word into its constituent phonemes so that the children can hear them, e.g. *pat – p-a-t*. Children can be asked to take turns to pull down the graphemes that represent the phonemes within words, saying the sound with each grapheme and ending by blending the sounds together to say the word – just as the teacher has modelled. This process needs to be repeated a number of times. This will ensure that children who are not confident can hear the sounds before they attempt to blend.

As children say the sounds, it is helpful to encourage children to point to the graphemes on their white boards. Some teachers find that the physical pushing of the graphemes together as children say the phonemes provides a physical representation of the aural blending activity. Children need to repeat the process until they can hear the sounds and blend them together (even if at this stage the child is merely copying rather than blending independently). It is important to remember that children are learning at this stage rather than independently applying their skills. Once they know the word, it is important to revisit it regularly until the children can read the word effortlessly.

Commentary

Assisted blending is not a feature of many phonics programmes, but it is a useful step in moving children towards independence. It is interesting to note when assessing children in Reception and Year 1 that many know their grapheme–phoneme correspondences but are unable to use them to read because they have not mastered the skill of blending – sometimes because they haven't been explicitly taught the process. Of course, there are many children who seem to be able to blend without ever having been taught. Often these children have had rich language experiences and are used to playing with the sounds within words.

Independent blending

As children become confident with assisted blending, the teacher should begin to notice that some children do not need the teacher's heavy modelled scaffold to blend the sounds into words. It is important as a teacher, therefore, to continuously assess as part of normal classroom teaching (so assessment for learning), listening to children as they see new words presented as part of the phonics lesson and importantly, when children are learning in free flow play or are engaged in independent learning across the curriculum. This careful observation ensures that the teacher is able to match teaching to children's needs.

Some children will quickly be able to hear how sounds become words from modelling previous assisted blending; others will take longer. As children grow in confidence with sounds they know, they will begin to explore blending on their own and it is important to provide opportunities across the curriculum for children to be able to do this. The planned, rich, literate learning environment is essential here. This, too, is where children will be able to make the link between phonics teaching and the purpose of phonics teaching. Children need a purpose for the application of phonics learning and cross-curricular learning makes reading and writing purposeful.

In addition to these planned opportunities the teacher needs to follow children's interests and be prepared to follow up incidental learning opportunities. In addition, to build children's confidence, it is helpful to keep word cards of previously taught CVC words and use these for games and activities. This will encourage children to consolidate their learning and develop rapid and effortless decoding. It is important, however, to remember that while decontextualised word cards or flash cards, as they are sometimes known, can have their uses, it is more important to support children in applying their blending skills in the real context of reading.

Children's literature

Having a literature-rich environment is essential in a primary school, especially during Early Years (Rose, 2006). Children need to be exposed to books and print at an early age. This encourages them to develop a love of reading. Having books with few words will draw upon their experiences and encourage children to make up their own stories. Children need to identify reading as important. Noticing that teachers and teaching assistants are readers and seeing a variety of print will encourage children to regard reading as purposeful and pleasurable. Reading a wide variety of books will allow children to form opinions, preferences and have an understanding of the structures and patterns of stories. Regularly reading to children and discussing stories, poems and songs will not only develop their enthusiasm for reading, but it will also give you opportunities to focus on sounds and interesting words.

Introducing pseudo words

Pseudo words have become increasingly important since the introduction of the Year 1 Phonics Screening Check. These are words that cannot be found in the dictionary, because they are not real words, but are phonically regular. They are used to check on children's ability to decode using phonic skills. Using pseudo words in lessons ensures that children understand how to blend and are not simply able to read words because they are familiar with them or have developed a sight vocabulary rather than the skill of blending to read. When they are experimenting with word building using restricted numbers of letters such as *s,a,t,p,i,n*, they will often create phonically plausible 'words' which do not actually exist. This will also ensure that children have confidence using pseudo words in Year 1.

Commentary

It is important to remember that the use of pseudo words, particularly in the Year 1 Phonics Screening Check, is highly contested. Look at the UK Literacy Association (UKLA) website (UKLA, 2012) to identify some of the arguments against the use of pseudo words. However, as there are no plans for the screening check to change, it is helpful to prepare children in ways that provide a context for the decoding of pseudo words (see Chapter 5 for further suggestions).

Case study

Reception teacher, Sidra, introduced alien puppets to her class. The children named these puppets using pseudo words. When children were reading or writing pseudo words, they used the alien to help them blend the words. When using word cards in the writing area, children were able to sort real words and nonsense words using the aliens. The children were able to use these puppets as they went up to Year 1, and many of the children who lacked confidence in the Phonics Screening Check used the puppets as support tools.

Role play

Role play is a central part of children's Early Years' experience. Role play allows children to model what they have been taught in class. If children are independently blending and showing early signs of writing, then you have created a literature-rich environment and have promoted a love of reading and writing. It is important that children can relate to the role play area and know how to use it, i.e. if your role play links to the topic of jungles, you will need to model writing or reading within this scenario to help children gain sufficient knowledge to be able to take part in role play activities about jungles.

When using school role plays children are more likely to know how this relates as the teaching of reading occurs daily; they will model taught lessons and often mimic the teacher. For this reason, teachers need to play in the role play area with children, modelling the language and activity of the area. This provides children with extended opportunities for talk and models sustained shared thinking.

Case study

In Bob's Reception class, one of the most popular role plays was set up as the phonics section of the classroom. Children had registers, an alphabet frieze and identical cards to the teachers. Children loved playing the role of the teacher. Most importantly, children were able to model using clear sounds (not adding the *schwa* to the end of sounds), assisted blending, and were enthusiastic when 'teaching'. It was clear that children knew the importance of reading and knew what they were learning.

Teaching your class

Activities/tasks

The key to encourage children to blend independently is to make it enjoyable. Encourage them by using words previously taught. This will give children confidence and result in higher participation, particularly during Child Initiated Play. You might include the following.

- Blending using high-frequency decodable word cards in the reading/writing area; cards children can use to role play as teacher.

- Using magnetic letters on white boards to allow children to create words to blend. This does not rely on them forming letters, which can slow many children down.

- Labelled cups and ping-pong balls with letters. Children place ping-pong balls into the cups (you can differentiate this according to learning need). They can use real words or nonsense words. If they are struggling to blend, they can identify the sound as they place it in the cup. Encouraging children to record the words they have been able to read will raise productivity.

- Racing car blending (using a phoneme frame). When playing during Child Initiated Play, place letters on top of cars. As children park the cars in the car park, encourage children to blend the sounds (this could be the fee to exit the car park, or a secret code word).

- Using play dough cutters, children make words (CVC) and read these. Children could take pictures of these words and they could be displayed on the white board the next day for children to read. This will ensure children are engaged in the task they should be completing.

Main lesson

This lesson is taught using the format of Letters and Sounds, with children working within Phase 2. It is assumed that they have completed Week 1 (they know the sounds *s,a,t,p*) and are moving on to Week 2.

Revisit and review

Practise previously learnt letters – this could be with flash cards or children identifying sounds on a white board using magnetic letters. Alphabet fans can be used so that children can show you the letters that represent the sounds you say.

Practise oral blending and segmentation based on words you have previously read. As children learn words through assisted blending, write them on cards and revise these daily so that children store these in their memories. As they do this more often, they should be able to read the word instantly.

Review the words *sat, tap, pat*. Children should be able to read these words with the teacher pointing to the sounds within the word.

Teach

Introduce the letter *i* – to engage children make up a story using props. For example, if you have a class bear/puppet you could introduce the sound by saying *Jeffrey has been playing in the garden today, shall we go and find him?* As the children walk outside, they find Jeffrey the bear under a tree with an insect. Introduce the insect to the children: *Look children, Jeffrey has a friend; he is an insect.* Encourage the children to repeat this word. Can children guess the sound they will be learning?

Say the sound to children, encouraging them to repeat the sound /i/. Show them pictures with the initial sound /i/, for example: *igloo, insect, infant, in.* Ask children to repeat these words and discuss their meaning. Can they make silly sentences using these words, for example: *Insects live in igloos.* Can children think of any words that have the initial sound /i/?

Practise

Practise reading and/or spelling words with the new letter, for example, *pin, pit, sit, tip*. Sound buttons help to visually support children when blending. Point to the sounds and repeat, assisting children with blending (if necessary), and encouraging them to copy you if they cannot hear the sounds within the word. As you practise these words, keep showing them the whole word to see if they can remember the word.

Apply

Children should now be able to blend with your help, using one or more phonically regular high-frequency words. Try: *Today we are going to write 'pin'.* Model with children how to do this, identifying the number of sounds within a word. Children should be able to segment this word and hear the sounds you have taught them. Together, write the words (it may be helpful for some children to use magnetic letters, as then they do not have to worry about letter formation if they struggle with fine motor skills). Once they have written the phrase, repeat it and read it from the board.

Extension/child initiated learning

Children need to be able to explore using the skills they have been taught throughout the day. This will help them to grow in confidence and practise the skills they have been taught. Place the words they have been reading around the sand tray, for example: *sat, tap, pat, pin, sit, tip*. Place letters in the sand tray and ask children to explore in the sand tray to find and then read the words. You may also want to ask children to write the words, but the focus of the early stages of phonics needs to be on reading rather than spelling and letter formation.

It is also helpful to give the reading a purpose The words could be part of clues left by some pirates and you only find the treasure if you follow the instructions, so children have to 'tap' the 'hat' and then 'tip' the sand onto the 'mat'. They can tick off all of the clues and actions they have carried out before the hiding place of the treasure is revealed!

Once the phonic lesson is complete, place the words they have learnt in a pocket chart or on a word wall. This will mean children can review these words. Many children enjoy writing these on white boards or in chalk.

Supporting Key Stage 2 children who have difficulties blending

Children who enter Key Stage 2 not being able to blend successfully will continue to need support and guidance. For some, this will be due to learning difficulties and a lack of enthusiasm may be preventing them from making progress. They will need a structured programme delivered by an experienced teacher to ensure rapid progress.

It is essential that the programme is not a repeat of phonic delivery they had in Key Stage 1. The intervention must have a good pace and not be patronising – many phonics books are very simple and can become boring for older children. It can make them feel anxious looking at books their peers are reading and this can discourage them from wanting to learn.

It is important that children learn sounds at a good pace and are not held back once they are beginning to blend. Children will need to revise sounds throughout the day through short, sharp revision sessions. There are many programmes available. For further information about what works in terms of catch-up programmes the Education Endowment Fund provides a comprehensive 'Toolkit'. This can be found at: **http:// educationendowmentfoundation.org.uk/toolkit/toolkit-a-z.**

Support for Spelling is also widely used and follows this model.

- Teach, model, define: this is where the teacher would model blending.

- Practise, explore, investigate: children independently apply the skills taught. This could be in a group or as an independent task.

- Apply, assess, reflect: children reflect upon what they have been able to achieve; they will blend and segment simple words.

Case study

Wayne entered Year 4 knowing very few sounds. Although English was his first language, he had lived abroad and had not been exposed to written print. He was unable to blend and did not enjoy reading. He attended phonics classes with Year 1 for one term and had additional one-to-one support in the afternoon for 15 minutes with an experienced teacher. After one term, he was able to blend most words and able to read most tricky words. Although he needed some support in class, he was able to enter Year 4 being able to read and write most words. He needed to break words into syllables to read, but was able to attempt reading most words. While working in Year 1 he was able to gain confidence and believed in his ability to read and write. He is now on track to reach Level 4 during Year 6.

Learning outcomes review

You should now be able to identify strategies to support teaching young children phonemes and identify potential barriers to learning and reflect upon ways to overcome these.

Answers to CVC words activity (page 39)

- *dock, shop, pig, badge, watch* are CVC words because each has a single consonant sound at the beginning followed by a single vowel sound followed by a single consonant sound.

- *day* and *boy* have a consonant sound followed by a vowel sound, but no final consonant sound (/d/ay/ and /b/oy/) and so are not CVC words.

- *free* has two consonant sounds followed by a vowel sound (/f/r/ee/) and so is not a CVC word.

- *steep* has two consonant sounds followed by a vowel sound, followed by a consonant sound (/s/t/ee/p/) and so is not a CVC word.

- *help* has a consonant sound followed by a vowel sound, followed by two consonant sounds (/h/e/l/p/) and so is not a CVC word.

References

Department for Children, Schools and Families (DCSF) (2009) *Support for Spelling*. London: DCSF.

Department for Education (DfE) (2013a) *The National Curriculum in England: Framework Document*. London: DfE.

Department for Education (DfE) (2013b) *Early Years Outcomes*. A non-statutory guide for practitioners and inspectors to help inform understanding of child development through the early years. Available at: **www.gov.uk/government/publications** [accessed 6 April 2015].

Department for Education and Skills (DfES) (2007) *Letters and Sounds: Principles and Practice of High Quality Phonics*. London: DfES.

Miskin, R (2011) *Read Write Inc.: Phonics Handbook*. Oxford: Oxford University Press.

Rose, J (2006) *The Independent Review of the Teaching of Early Reading*. London: DCSF.

UK Literacy Association (UKLA) (2012) *Phonics Screening Check Fails a Generation of Able Readers*. Available at: **www.ukla.org/news/story/phonics_screening_check_fails_a_generation_of_able_readers** [accessed 5 April 2015].

www.mrthorne.com/or – *Mr Thorne Does Phonics* [accessed 19 December 2014].

Chapter 5

Year 1: Teaching grapheme–phoneme correspondences

Learning outcomes

This chapter explores how children learn to represent phonemes with graphemes. It looks at how children can use the process of segmenting spoken words into sounds before choosing graphemes to represent the sounds.

This chapter will allow you to achieve the following outcomes:

- develop an understanding of what children need to know about using graphemes;
- identify engaging ways in which graphemes can be taught;
- have a greater awareness of how to teach children to identify and use graphemes to write words.

Teachers' Standards

Working through this chapter will help you meet the following standards:

2. Promote good progress and outcomes by pupils:

- Be aware of pupils' capabilities and their prior knowledge, and plan teaching to build on these.

3. Demonstrate good subject and curriculum knowledge:

- Demonstrate an understanding of and take responsibility for promoting high standards of literacy, articulacy and the correct use of standard English, whatever the teacher's specialist subject.

4. Plan and teach well-structured lessons:

- Impart knowledge and develop understanding through effective use of lesson time.

Links to the National Curriculum

Key Stage 1 statutory requirement

Year 1

The boundary between revision of work covered in Reception and the introduction of new work may vary according to the programme used, but basic revision should include:

- all letters of the alphabet and the sounds which they most commonly represent, consonant digraphs which have been taught and the sounds which they represent;
- vowel digraphs which have been taught and the sounds which they represent;
- the process of segmenting spoken words into sounds before choosing graphemes to represent the sounds;
- words with adjacent consonants;
- guidance and rules which have been taught.

(DfE, 2013, p50)

Key focus: Teaching grapheme–phoneme correspondences (GPCs)

With the introduction of the Phonics Screening Check in 2012, it is fundamental that children in Year 1 are able to *decode to an appropriate standard* (DFE, 2013). With many phonics programmes available, it is essential that phonics is taught explicitly and is well organised and sequenced. It should cover all common grapheme–phoneme correspondences in the English language and all 40+ phonemes and their alternative spellings and pronunciations need to be taught and applied in reading and writing. Alongside this, we need to teach high-frequency words and words with irregular spellings (common exception words) such as *the, was, one, why, who* and *said* (see Chapter 11).

A grapheme is a letter or a number of letters that represent a sound (phoneme) in a word. A digraph is two letters which make one phoneme, so in *chip ch* is a consonant digraph which represents a single sound (phoneme), and in *feet* /ee/ is a vowel digraph which represents one phoneme. When three letters represent one sound, as /tch/ does in *match* and /igh/ does in *high*, this is called a 'trigraph'. English has some instances of four letters representing one sound, including /ough/ in *though* and /augh/ in *caught*: these are known as 'quadgraphs'.

Activity: Identifying digraphs, trigraphs and quadgraphs

Look at the words below and then answer the questions:

watch   height   wish   bridge   cheap   much   plough

- Which words end with a consonant digraph?
- Which words include a quadgraph?
- Which words have a consonant trigraph?
- Which word has a consonant digraph and a vowel digraph?

Essential set-up

All staff working in your classroom will need to remember that the application of phonics runs throughout the curriculum. Children need to have adults who are good models, demonstrating the application of phonics in reading and writing for a range of audiences and purposes across the curriculum. Reading and writing should be held in high regard throughout the curriculum and not just taught during explicit phonics lessons. A print-rich environment will support children to apply their phonics knowledge and use the skills they have been taught in phonics lessons.

Classroom displays should support children's learning, and could include a phoneme–grapheme chart which shows the most common representations for each of the 44 phonemes; 'tricky words' that children are learning to read and write (these can be taken from the National Curriculum); writing checklists or reminders of what they need to include in their writing, for example punctuation, capital letters for names and to begin sentences and vocabulary lists, to enhance children's writing. Children's work displayed for other National Curriculum subjects should sustain the standard of writing seen in literacy books.

Parents' and carers' meetings

Parents and carers are the most influential adults in children's lives and so they should be the focus of partnership working in the teaching of reading. The more parents feel involved, the more likely they are to feel able to ask questions and provide the class teacher with information about a child's home literacy practices that can support the set-up of the classroom and school provision. Parents and carers need to know they are a valued and indeed essential part of the learning process. The role that is most important is the parent supporting and maintaining a child's interest and motivation to read.

This means asking parents to continue to read to their child throughout Key Stage 1 and beyond. Some parents appreciate support with book choices, and so the class teacher should try and maintain and develop their knowledge of children's literature to facilitate this. High-quality texts give children access to the pleasure and purpose of reading as well as to enriched vocabulary, story structures and patterns and the organisation and structures of non-fiction text. This is perhaps the most significant role that parents can play, particularly as this aspect of teaching reading has not changed over the years.

Modelling

Teachers can help parents and carers by modelling how children are taught in school. This can ensure children are given the same messages at home and at school. It is helpful to give parents a little subject knowledge, including the terminology that is used in the school. It is also helpful to demonstrate the articulation of the sounds; how to identify sounds within words and how key teaching approaches are used; for example, how to use phoneme frames. Demonstrate the importance of blending and how you identify sounds within a word and thus segmenting for spelling.

It may be useful to show them how children identify sounds by placing a dot for single sounds and a dash for digraphs, trigraphs and quadgraphs. Many successful schools invite parents to learn alongside their children as part of a normal phonics lesson, as well as offering separate workshops for parents at the start of Year 1 and at key points through the year. Clearly, it is important that teachers liaise with colleagues in the Foundation Stage to ensure that messages to parents and carers are consistent and are progressive as their children move through the school.

There are many different phonics programmes used in schools, and schools may change the programme they use over a number of years. Because programmes can vary in the order sounds are taught and how they are taught, it is helpful to make the scheme used, or changes to the scheme used, clear for parents. This avoids confusion, particularly where a parent has a number of children moving through the school or in different schools. It can be helpful for parents to be given the order in which grapheme–phoneme correspondences are taught in school, so that they can support their children without confusing them. Children are usually the best teachers of their parents, so encourage children to show their parents how they use sounds to read and write.

Enunciation

A key element of successful teaching and learning of phonics is clear enunciation. It can be very confusing for children if letters are sounded with the addition of a *schwa* sound, so that instead of sounding letters like *f* as *fff*, and *l* as *lll* they are sounded as *fuh* and *luh*. This can lead to misconceptions and misspellings, with children writing things like 'ft' for 'foot' because they can hear a vowel sound at the end of *f*, and 'bt' for 'butter' and 'cl' for 'colour'.

For both teachers and other adults who support children's early reading, it is essential that phonemes are enunciated cleanly and with minimal additional vowel sounds. This is easy for letters such as *a,c,e,f,h,I,l,m,n*, but more difficult for letters such as *b* and *p*. Letters and Sounds (DfES, 2007) includes a DVD which shows a mouth as each phoneme is sounded cleanly, and it can be helpful to watch this while testing your enunciation.

Commentary

For parents and carers, who may have learned phonemes with the additional schwa *sound, some coaching and light-hearted activities may help.*

Teaching sequences for grapheme–phoneme correspondences

Below you will find charts showing the sequence of grapheme–phoneme correspondences for each of the three most commonly used systematic synthetic phonics programmes: Jolly Phonics, Letters and Sounds, and Read Write Inc. (Miskin, 2011).

Table 5.1 Grapheme–phoneme correspondences

Jolly Phonics	Week
s a t i p	1
n c/k e h r	2
m d g o u	3
l f b ai j	4
oa ie ee or z w	5
ng v oo oo y x	6
ch sh th th qu ou	7
oi ue er ar	8

Letters and Sounds	
s a t p	Phase 2 (Reception)
i n m d	
g o c k	
ck e u r	
h b f, ff l, ll ss	

(Continued)

Table 5.1 (Continued)

Letters and Sounds	
j v w x	Phase 3 (Reception)
y z, zz qu	
ch, sh, th/th, ng, ai, ee, igh, oa, oo/oo, ar, or, ur, ow, oi, ear, air, ure, er*	
No new GPCs taught in this phase	Phase 4
Learn new phoneme /zh/ (in words like *treasure*)	Phase 5 (Year 1)

* 'er' represents a *schwa* (*uh*) sound as in *mother*.

Read Write Inc.	Group
m a s d t	1
i n p g o	2
c k u b	3
f e l h sh r	4
j v y w	5
th z ch qu x ng nk	6
ay ee igh ow oo oo ar or air ir ou oy	7
ire ear ure	8

N.B. The underlined letters are not single phonemes: nk (ngk), qu (cw), x (cs), ue (yoo).

High-frequency words/word lists

These lists support parents in identifying words that children should be able to read and write. It is helpful to be clear as a teacher which words are phonically regular and high frequency, for example *had*, and which words are high frequency but are 'tricky', where part of the word does not follow a regular phonics pattern. It is useful to share this with parents and carers and to provide guidance on strategies to help children learn them (see Chapter 11). Children should be able to identify the graphemes within these words to be able to read and write them confidently.

How children learn to represent phonemes with graphemes

The National Curriculum states that children in Year 1 should be able to *respond speedily with the correct sound to graphemes (letters or groups of letters) for all 40+ phonemes, including, where applicable, alternative sounds for graphemes* (DfE, 2013).

Below are some activities that support children in learning the phoneme–grapheme correspondences.

Grapheme flowers

Place the grapheme for the sound in the centre of the flower, for example *ay*. Children then need to think of words to place on the 'petals' around the outside; for example, *day, stay, play, crayon, way*. This could be an independent activity for reviewing their knowledge.

Literature

Having books that children can read independently in a class library will encourage them to apply the phonics skills that have been taught and will foster a love of reading. Display book covers and extracts from books that are easily decodable, so that children can enjoy reading them and will want to read the whole books.

Dot and dash

Place words on the board with sounds the children know and ask them to work together to 'dot and dash' them, with dots under single graphemes and dashes under digraphs, trigraphs and quadgraphs. This will show you if they are able to identify sounds within a word, and if they can do this they should be able to blend the sounds to read the word.

Real or pseudo words?

Write words on cards and ask children to read the words and sort them according to real words and pseudo words. Some might use dictionaries to check if they are right. Pseudo words feature in the Year 1 Phonics Screening Check and are often highlighted as the most contentious part of the check. The government claims that the decoding of pseudo words enables teachers to assess a child's phonics skills and knowledge, context free. Children have to read the words using only their decoding skills and cannot rely on the context of the sentence or whole word, sight knowledge when reading pseudo words.

This can present difficulties for some children, as they have been taught (rightly) to check what they have read makes sense. Therefore, some children can read a pseudo word and then change their reading to a word that is similar but is a real word, in an attempt to make sense of what they have been asked to decode. For the purposes of real reading this is an important step, but for the purposes of the Screening Check it can cause difficulties (see the commentary section below).

For this reason, it is helpful to give pseudo words some sort of context and purpose. It is helpful to ask children to create or design, at the start of the year, a drawing or painting of a monster and/or an alien and/or a strange fish or sea creature. These can then be displayed and named by the teacher – naming each of the creatures with a pseudo word. There is then some point to decoding these words; after all, the children will want to know what the creatures are called! The section below about the book *Welcome to Alien School* (Hart, 2012) is useful when teaching pseudo words.

Finding the sound

Give children sentences or a short paragraph (according to their current attainment) and ask them to identify the words that include a specific sound, for example /ay/. Ask children to ensure they have read the passage aloud all the way through and have not simply scanned to identify the sound without reading the text.

This is important because children need to see that learning grapheme–phoneme correspondences is not an end in itself, and that this knowledge and understanding will enable them to read for meaning. Once children have located these words, see if they can put them into sentences. Try and make sure if you do this that there is some sort of purpose to the sentences; whenever children are asked to write, they need to see it as purposeful and to have some point beyond doing it for the teacher.

Main lesson

Learning the 'ee' sound

Introduce the sound

As children learn a bank of sounds, they will be able to recall previous sounds. As they do this, it is helpful to collate the graphemes that make the same sounds. This is useful for children to refer to when writing. So for the 'ee' sound you may find they suggest words where the sound is made by *ea* (*beat*), *e-e* (*these*), *ie* (*belief*) or *ei* (*receive*).

When showing the children a sound it can be helpful to introduce a phrase (this could be accompanied by a picture). Children may often remember the phrase or picture, which will prompt them to remember the sound. Introduce *ee* using a picture of a sheep labelled: 'feed the sheep'. This could be accompanied by a picture of a farmer feeding his or her herd. As children say this, they can pretend to bend down and feed sheep.

Ensure that children can identify the letters that make the sound. It will support the children to have the picture and the grapheme that represents the sound printed in the classroom; this ensures that if children can remember the phrase they can find how to write the sound they need. At this stage, children will need to know letter names as well as sounds. They need this knowledge as they have to be able to distinguish the 'ee' sound made by double *e* and that made by an *e* and an *a*, for example.

Listen to and use the sound in context

Children will need to hear words that contain the 'ee' sound. As you say words that contain the sound, for example *tree, meet, jeep, seeds, sweets*, say the words using sound buttons, for example:

t r ee

Ask children to blend the sounds together to make a word. It is useful for children to put these words into context and to talk about the meaning of words. It is essential to keep in mind the purpose of phonics – to enable children to read for meaning – and so at every instance teachers need to connect decoding with vocabulary comprehension and meaning. Children who have English as an additional language (EAL) may need pictures to support them once they have decoded a word. This enables them to extend their English vocabulary knowledge.

Phonics programmes often use rather unusual words, even for children who have English as a first language, because they are limited in their grapheme choices to the phonics phase being taught. For this reason all children, regardless of first language or attainment, may need additional support with word meanings. You will need to provide examples of these to support their understanding.

Applying the sound: Reading the 'ee' sound

Children should now be able to read words containing the 'ee' sound. It is helpful to display these for all to see. When introducing the sound, it helps to include sound buttons underneath. This supports children to clearly identify the 'ee' sound within a word. It will also help them to focus on applying the sound you are learning, for example, *sh-ee-p*. They will then need to blend those sounds to make a word.

As children revise reading words, they will begin to store them in their *orthographic memory*. This means that they will then remember the word and will not need continually to sound it out. This will support their fluency while reading. To do this, it may be helpful to write the words as flash cards or display them in your classroom. It is always important to include in teaching some application of reading a new grapheme in a meaningful context. This could be an appropriate decodable text or a caption or sentence to accompany something the class is working on, including labels and signs for the classroom.

Writing the 'ee' sound

As you say the sounds of words, it will support children to count the number of sounds within a word, for example *s-ee-d-s*. Children should count that there are four sounds and check that they have four sounds after they write the word. They will need to repeat the sounds within a word when initially learning to use the 'ee' sound. It will support lower attaining children to show them the sound buttons as they are writing the word.

> ### Commentary
>
> *It may help children if you say the sounds in different voices, as this will help them to remember the sounds they are writing. Try using high and low voices and even different accents and encourage children to do the same. This can make the activity more engaging and interactive as well as emphasising clean enunciation.*

Assessment

Check children have written the word correctly; if they have not, encourage them to write out the graphemes again. Once children know one way of writing one sound, higher attaining children should be able to identify alternative graphemes to represent the phoneme, for example *ea* for the 'ee' sound.

Check children's ability to use the right graphemes for the sounds you have been teaching that week in an informal spelling test. Spelling tests allow you to identify if children can apply the sounds they have learnt independently.

When children are writing in other lessons, you will be able to identify which sounds they can confidently use, and you will be able to assess which sounds they need to revise based on their spelling. You will need to encourage children to check the graphemes they use in all lessons; their writing should be of the same standard in literacy lessons and other lessons within school.

Welcome to Alien School: Using nonsense/pseudo words

When teaching a grapheme, you might use Caryl Hart's book *Welcome to Alien School* to teach nonsense words or to introduce nonsense words to your class.

Introduction
Introduce the story and show children bits of the text.

When, one morning, Mum calls Albie for school, he really doesn't want to go; he's too busy playing space rescues with his toys. But, when Albie steps into the playground, he quickly realises that this isn't any old school. He meets a large alien who soon becomes his friend.

Development
When in the classroom, the aliens are taking a spelling test. Albie hasn't heard of these words before and is worried about spelling them, but we are going to help him! In this part of the book the examples given to spell are: *bazoozle-squark, flobbedy-obbedy-pompom* and *tog-tog, de-noggle-plomp*. You could change these words for your children and ask them to take an 'alien spelling test', which should use the grapheme that you have taught that morning, for example *ay – shray, glay, wray*.

As you say the words, ask children to identify the sounds within the words, placing 'sound buttons' under the graphemes. You could also introduce 'human' words as a spelling contrast, for example: *day, say, play, crayon*. Encourage children to write these, comparing the words and identifying the focus grapheme. Can they use the human words within a sentence? Could they think of a definition for the alien words?

In the book, the aliens have names, for example *Nogel*. Replace the aliens' names with their own choices of alien names, using the chosen grapheme (this could also be an opportunity to revise previously taught graphemes by using them within the aliens' names). Ask children to write these on the board, placing sound buttons underneath to show that they can identify the sounds within a word.

In the book, the aliens visit the school canteen – place this page under the visualiser or scan in the picture and add labels to the food and see if the children can read the words using the 'ay' sound.

Extension
Children could make a dictionary of alien language. This could be built upon as you teach sounds. It might take the form of a book or it could be a wall dictionary.

Encourage children to make up their own names for aliens and their own alien words, and check to see if they use appropriate grapheme–phoneme correspondences.

Commentary

There is some controversy about the teaching of pseudo words, with some teachers finding that able readers misread them because they tried to make them into real alternatives, for example reading 'brudge' as 'bridge' and 'frind' as 'friend'. Others question the value of children focusing on such words when they could be spending more time on real words. However, as the Phonics Screening Test requires children to read pseudo words to check their decoding skills, teachers will continue to focus on them. The alien activity at least makes exploring pseudo words meaningful as it gives children opportunities to name characters.

Pseudo words: An alternative approach to check phonemic knowledge

Instead of using invented words, you can check children's phonic strategies by asking them to read phonically regular place names. This is a more meaningful activity and can be developed into purposeful cross-curricular work.

Choose an appropriate selection from the town names in Table 5.2 and ask children to read as many as possible and check to see if they apply their phonemic awareness.

Table 5.2   English place names

Abingdon	Acton	Amble
Bakewell	Barking	Bridlington
Burnley	Catford	Chester
Chesterfield	Chorley	Crawley
Diss	Droitwich	Exmouth
Frant	Fleetwood	Glossop
Grantham	Grays	Halifax
Howden	Ipswich	Jarrow
Kettering	Knutsford	Leek
Louth	Oakham	Otley
Oxford	Pocklington	Royston
Skegness	Queen's Park	Stroud
Tavistock	Tenby	Uckfield
Ventnor	Wells	Whitby
Whitehill	Yarmouth	Yate

What to look for:

- Do children read some words in one go without segmenting and blending?

- Do they adopt phonic strategies by breaking words up into individual phonemes?

- Can they spot digraphs?

- Do they break some words up into words within words, e.g. White/hill, Bake/well?

- Which grapheme–phoneme correspondences do they know well?

- Which GPCs do they struggle with?

- Give them some other towns to spell – try phonically regular ones. How do they manage?

What can you do next?

- Create a map with roads, rivers, perhaps the sea, railway lines, towns and villages.

- Decide on names for the different places – make them up.

- Discuss how these could be spelled.

- Try out different ways of spelling the names to see which seems most appropriate.

- Decide on a name for the whole area.

- When the map is drawn and labelled, ask questions such as: *How would you get from Oxby to Farlow?* These are designed to check the child can read the names and to see which strategies s/he uses to do this.

- If appropriate, talk about points of the compass, etc.

- Work together to write some sentences about the area and its attractions – you can add these as you go along.

Commentary

This activity can be adapted for different ages and abilities. Besides using place names and maps, you might use league tables and football results to engage older children.

Teaching Key Stage 2 children who may need support

When teaching Key Stage 2 children who need support, this can be done in the same way as teaching Key Stage 1, although you will need to change the words so that they are age appropriate. For example, when teaching the 'ee' sound you could use the words *redeem, indeed, oversee, feeble*. You might also engage their interest by using names of TV programmes, football teams and pop musicians, such as Coronation Str<u>ee</u>t, <u>Ea</u>stEnders, Chels<u>ea</u>, Qu<u>ee</u>ns Park Rangers, Cl<u>ea</u>n Bandit and Ed Sh<u>ee</u>ran.

It is important that you discuss with children any unfamiliar grapheme–phoneme correspondences that may arise when reading words. For example, for *feeble* you should identify that /le/ is one sound, just as it is in *little* and *bottle*, and you should explain this to them, sharing other examples which they are familiar with. Revising previously taught sounds daily is essential, and should be done throughout the day in short sharp bursts to ensure children do not always need to blend the sounds, but start to read them instantly.

As children move up the school, they will increasingly need to identify prefixes and suffixes and this will need to be addressed within intervention groups (see Chapter 8).

Learning outcomes review

You should now have an understanding of what children need to know about using graphemes and be able to devise engaging ways in which grapheme-phoneme correspondences can be taught. You should also have a greater awareness of how to teach children to identify and use graphemes to write words.

Answers to digraphs, trigraphs and quadgraphs activity (page 50)

- These words end with a consonant digraph – *wi<u>sh</u>, mu<u>ch</u>*

- These words include a quadgraph – *h<u>eigh</u>t, pl<u>ough</u>*

- These words have a consonant trigraph – *wa<u>tch</u>, bri<u>dge</u>*

- This word has a consonant digraph and a vowel digraph – <u>ch</u><u>ea</u>p

Further reading

Glazzard, J and Stokoe, J (2013) *Teaching Systematic Synthetic Phonics and Early English*. London: Critical Publishing.

See Chapter 5 for practical ideas on creative approaches to teaching systematic synthetic phonics.

Jolliffe, W (2007) *You Can Teach Phonics*. Leamington Spa: Scholastic.

Provides practical guidance on teaching phonics.

OFSTED (2014) *Getting Them Reading Early*. Distance learning materials for inspecting reading. London: DfE.

Provides examples of multisensory teaching on film.

References

Department for Education (DfE) (2013) *The National Curriculum in England: Framework Document*. London: DfE.

Department for Education and Skills (DfES) (2007) *Letters and Sounds: Principles and Practice of High Quality Phonics*. London: DfES.

Hart, C (2012) *Welcome to Alien School*. New York: Simon and Schuster.

Miskin, R (2011) *Read Write Inc.: Phonics Handbook*. Oxford: Oxford University Press.

Chapter 6

Year 1: Long vowel digraphs

Learning outcomes

This chapter will allow you to achieve the following outcomes:

- understand the features of the advanced alphabetic code;
- develop an understanding of long vowel digraphs;
- have an overview of how these phonemes can be taught in appropriate ways.

Teachers' Standards

Working through this chapter will help you meet the following standards:

3. Demonstrate good subject and curriculum knowledge:

- Demonstrate an understanding of and take responsibility for promoting high standards of literacy, articulacy and the correct use of standard English, whatever the teacher's specialist subject.
- If teaching early reading, demonstrate a clear understanding of systematic synthetic phonics.

4. Plan and teach well-structured lessons:

- Contribute to the design and provision of an engaging curriculum within the relevant subject area(s).

5. Adapt teaching to respond to the strengths and needs of all pupils:

- Know when and how to differentiate appropriately, using approaches which enable pupils to be taught effectively.

Links to the National Curriculum

Year 1

SPELLING
The boundary between revision of work covered in Reception and the introduction of new work may vary according to the programme used, but basic revision should include:

- all letters of the alphabet and the sounds which they most commonly represent;
- consonant digraphs which have been taught and the sounds which they represent;
- vowel digraphs which have been taught and the sounds which they represent.

On pages 62–63, the National Curriculum (DfE, 2013) provides a table of vowel digraphs and trigraphs with rules and guidance and example words.

Key focus

One of the most complex aspects of teaching phonics involves children using and applying the long vowel phonemes and the multiple spelling choices that go with many of these. This chapter will review this complex part of the alphabetic code and present a range of strategies to teach it effectively.

English has what is known as a 'complex orthography' compared with many other languages such as Italian, Spanish or Finnish. While some languages have simple orthographies, with perhaps 24 phonemes being represented by a similar number of graphemes, English has around 44 phonemes which can be represented not only by the 26 individual letters of the alphabet, but also by combinations of these letters. There are around 175 common ways of representing the 44 phonemes in English, but it has been estimated that there are over 400 actual possibilities, some of which only occur in a few words (Crystal, 2005).

This makes learning to read and write in English more of a challenge than in many other languages. For example, in Finland, which has a highly regular alphabetic code, children do not start formal learning of reading until they are around seven years old, but most learn very quickly and by age ten or eleven are among the best readers in the world (PIRLS, 2011). McGuinness has argued that *there is no question that the high functional illiteracy rate in English-speaking countries is largely a product of our formidable spelling code and the way it is (or is not) taught* (2004, p41).

There are four key concepts to be aware of when teaching phonics:

1. Sounds/phonemes are represented by letters/graphemes. Every sound in every word is represented by a letter or combination of letters.

2. A phoneme can be represented by one or more letters, for example the phoneme /igh/ can be written as 'i-e' (in *wine*), 'igh' (in *might*), 'ie' (in *tie*), 'eigh' (in *height*) or 'y' (in *by*). A one-letter grapheme is called a 'graph', a two-letter grapheme a 'digraph', a three-letter grapheme a 'trigraph' and occasionally a four-letter grapheme (as in *weigh* = /w/eigh/) a 'quadgraph'.

3. The same phoneme can be represented (spelled) more than one way, as in /or/ spelled as 'or' in *for*, 'ore' in *more*, or 'aw' as in *jaw*, or 'oor' as in *floor*.

4. The same grapheme (spelling) may represent more than one phoneme, for example by the letter *c* which may make the sound /k/ in *cat* or /s/ in *city*.

We tend to begin teaching phonics by teaching letter–sound correspondences from the basic alphabetic code, offering children one spelling choice for each of the 40+ sounds. This is done incrementally in systematic schemes, with common individual letters taught first, followed by less common ones and then the most common digraphs. Once they have mastered the simple code, children are gradually introduced to the advanced code, which requires them to learn multiple spellings for each phoneme.

The advanced code includes the long vowel phonemes and can be challenging for teachers to teach and children to learn.

Vowel phonemes

English has around 24 consonant sounds and 20 vowel sounds. Besides the five short vowel sounds /a/, /e/, /i/, /o/, /u/, there are 14 long vowel phonemes (see Table 6.1 which shows their common spellings). The other vowel sound is the *schwa* phoneme /ə/ (an unstressed vowel sound which is close to the phoneme /u/). There are various spellings of this phoneme including: teacher, collar, doctor, the, alike. The *schwa* is said to be the most common sound in the language.

Different spellings for long vowel phonemes

Because there are alternative spellings for each phoneme, learning long vowel phonemes can be challenging. For example, the phoneme /oa/ can be written in the following ways:

oa – as in *coat*

ow – as in *grow*

oe – as in *toe*

o-e – as in *hope*

ough – as in *though*

Now look at Table 6.1, which shows the 14 long vowel phonemes and common ways in which they can be represented. The fact that there are at least two alternative spellings for each long vowel phoneme illustrates the challenge we face when teaching children to read and spell.

Table 6.1 Long vowel phonemes

Phonemes	Grapheme(s)	Common spellings
/ae/	ay, a-e, ai, a	play, take, snail, baby
/ee/	ee, ea, e	feel, heat, me
/ie/	ie, igh, y, i-e, i	tie, flight, my, bike, tiger
/oe/	oa, ow, o-e, o	float, slow, stone, nose

/ue/	ue, ew, u-e	due, grew, tune
/oo/	oo, ue	room, clue
/ow/	ow, ou	cow, loud
/oi/	oi, oy	coin, boy
/ur/	ur, ir, er, ear, or	fur, girl, term, heard, work
/au/	au, or, oor, ar, aw, a	sauce, horn, door, warn, claw, ball
/ar/	ar, a	car, fast (regional), ma, pa
/air/	air, ear, are	hair, bear, share
/ear/	ear, ere, eer	ear, here, deer
/ure/	ure, our	sure, tour

See Jolliffe and Waugh with Carss (2015, p55).

Long vowel phonemes usually contain digraphs (two letters making one sound, e.g. /ae/ written as 'ai' or 'ay' in *rain* and *way*) or trigraphs (three letters making one sound, e.g. /air/ in *pair* or *wear*). Occasionally, long vowel phonemes are represented by a single letter 'y', as in *try, fry, by* and *sty*, a single 'e' as in *me, be, he* and *she*, a single 'o' as in *go, so* and *no*, or a single 'a' as in *ma* and *pa*.

Activity: Identifying long vowel phonemes

Check your understanding of long vowel phonemes.

Look at the list of words below and see if you can identify those that contain long vowel phonemes:

rain	soap	rod	road	bit	bite
say	cat	write	by	tube	set
boy	shout	heat	met	hug	huge

When you are asked to use a systematic synthetic phonics programme, be sure to check the order in which long vowel digraphs are taught. For example, some programmes introduce the 'ow' digraph as the /oa/ sound in *show* and *know*, while others introduce it as the /ow/ sound in *now* and *how*.

Activity: Alternative spellings for long vowel phonemes

How many ways can you find to spell the phoneme /ee/ as in *meet*? (There are at least ten.)

Although the above activity may make you feel that learning to spell must be very difficult, if you look at some of the examples, you will find it difficult to find many other examples of words which use the same spelling pattern for the /ee/ sound.

We tend, therefore, to focus first on the most common spellings when teaching grapheme–phoneme correspondences. The other combinations may be taught as part of learning tricky or common exception words and when highlighting the 'tricky' parts of some words.

Teaching your class

Teaching long vowel phonemes can be a challenging task, and is most effective when taught in a lively and interactive manner. Below are some examples of how this can be accomplished.

Using actions

Jolly Phonics teaches children sounds using actions. Each phoneme is accompanied by a story that introduces an action. For example, the /t/ sound is made while turning your head from side to side as if watching a tennis match, while the /s/ sound is accompanied by moving your arm as if it is a snake. There are actions for long vowel sounds too, including cupping your hand to your ear for *ai*, as if saying *ay?* or *eh?*; and pretending to be a donkey with hands on head as ears while saying *ee* (or *eeyore*).

Using mnemonics

Read Write Inc. (Miskin, 2011) uses mnemonics when teaching phonemes. For example, when learning the sound /ae/ as in *day*, the children say the sound while looking at the written form 'ay'. Their phoneme revision cards have a picture printed on the back, which has a written mnemonic. When this is revealed, children say the phrase. For example, 'May I play?' This is repeated frequently and supports children in remembering the phoneme and common spellings.

Build a chart

To support children it is helpful to build a chart of phonemes as you teach each one. The most common graphemes for each phoneme need to be focused upon first. For example, words which end in the /ae/ sound are usually spelled with 'ay' – *day, way, say*, etc. Exceptions include *they, grey, sleigh*, but these words can be looked at as 'tricky' or 'common exception' words (see Chapter 11).

Words which have an /ae/ sound in the middle are often spelled with 'ai' – *rain, pain, again* – or with the split vowel digraph 'a-e' – *take, made, wake*. Again, there are exceptions, including *vein, straight, weight*, but the initial focus will be on those words that include 'ai' and 'ay'. See Table 6.2 below for an example of a long vowel phoneme chart.

Table 6.2 Long vowel phoneme chart

/ae/	/ee/	/ie/	/oe/	/u/	/ue/	/ow/	/oi/	/ur/	/au/	/ar/	/air/	/ear/	/ure/
ay (day)	ee (see)	ie (tie)	oa (boat)	oo (book)	oo (moon)	ow (cow)	oi (coin)	ur (burn)	au (autumn)	ar (car)	air (hair)	ear (fear)	ure (sure)
ai (tail)	ea (tea)	igh (night)	ow (snow)	ou (would)	ue (clue)	ou (shout)	oy (boy)	ir (girl)	or (horn)	a (fast)	ear (bear)	ere (here)	our (tour)
a (baby)	e (me)	y (my)	o (cold)	u (put)	ew (chew)			er (term)	oor (door)		are (share)	eer (hear)	
a-e (make)	y (pony)	i (tiger)	o-e (bone)		u-e (tune)			ear (heard)	ar (warm)				
		i-e (time)						or (work)	aw (saw)				
									a (call)				

See Jolliffe and Waugh with Carss (2015, p61).

Main lesson

Learning the 'ae' sound

This lesson will equip you to teach the sound 'ae', when it is represented by the graphemes /ay/ or /ai/. The lesson can be adapted to support the teaching of any long vowel digraph.

Introduce the sound 'ae'. Explain to the children that they are going to learn two ways of representing this sound in writing. Show children the grapheme and tell them that these two letters together make one sound and it is 'ay'. This should be taught alongside a phrase or mnemonic, for example, 'play this way' or 'I can stay away' or 'once again it's going to rain'. It may be helpful to add actions; for example, for 'once again it's going to rain', they could mime putting up an umbrella.

To support visual learning when introducing the sound, it may be helpful to write the sound on the board and then draw pictures to help children remember the phrase. For example, for 'once again it's going to rain', you could draw someone putting up an umbrella and a dark cloud overhead. It is important that children can clearly distinguish the sound and the phrase. Children should repeat after you saying the sound, using different voices, for example, a loud voice, quiet voice, singing voice, a whisper. This variation helps them to internalise the sound.

Hearing the sound in context
Children should hear the sound within a word, as this places it in context. First, say the words and ask the children to repeat them, for example, *may, pain, wait, pay*. As children say the words, encourage them to segment the words orally, for example, *p-ai-n*. Repeat this with each word. To reinforce the meaning of a word, put it into a sentence and then ask children to make up their own sentences orally, for example, *Wait until I say you can play*.

Read and write the sound
Write the words on cards for the children to read. Place dots (one letter making a sound) and dashes (two or more letters that make one sound) under the letters, as this will support children who cannot independently identify the sounds within a word. For example:

wait   may   sway

Encourage children to say the segmented sounds and then model how they blend together. For example, *ch-ai-n*, then repeat the word *chain*. Children should be able to blend the sounds independently; however, this will depend on their ability. Some may need support to blend sounds together to make words. If a child has reached this stage in his or her learning and is unable to blend independently, this becomes the priority.

Commentary

The skill of blending is central to reading and it must always be remembered that phonics is only being taught in order to develop reading. For this reason, it is a good idea to take away the dots and dashes on cards once children do not need this scaffold. If you always have dots and dashes, some children will rely on these prompts and may find it hard when reading independently and applying skills in story book reading.

It is also a good idea to withdraw the scaffold of sounding before blending. When children have read words a number of times using sounding and blending, encourage them to have a go at reading the whole word – automatically decoding. Avoid encouraging them to remember the whole word, but move children to automatic and rapid decoding as part of the process of removing the scaffolds on the journey to independent reading.

Review the lesson

At the end of the lesson, show children the graphemes 'ay' and 'ai' and encourage them to repeat the sound and some words that include them. You should be able to show them the words that contain the sound 'ae', and they should be able to read these. Recap these throughout the day, so that children are able to memorise these words. This will support their fluency in reading.

Development

Review the sound taught, saying the phrase or mnemonic. Show children the words you have taught them to read. It may be helpful to write these on cards to review throughout the day. Find opportunities in other lessons to draw attention to words that include the 'ae' sound.

Extension

If higher ability children are able to read the words easily, you could write more challenging sentences for them to read, for example, *Can you stay on Monday? One day I'm going to play football in Spain.* Children could also write their own sentences, using the words you have taught them to read.

Assessment

To assess if children are able to apply this sound, place written text on the board and encourage children to read it. This could also be printed and read with a partner.

You will need to identify which common exception or 'tricky' words the children have been taught, in order for the children to read sentences containing words using the 'ae' sound. For example, in order to construct sentences like *I love to stay out and play all day unless it rains*, they will need to know the common exception word *love*.

Commentary

Long vowel sounds can differ in different parts of the country. They tend to be one of the main indicators of a person's accent. Look at the following words and think how they might typically be pronounced by people from Newcastle, East Yorkshire, the Midlands, London, and the West Country: hope, pain, book, state.

Teaching Key Stage 2 children who may need support

Before teaching the vowel digraphs, you will have to assess children to identify the gaps in their knowledge. Children will need to learn these sounds at a steady pace to ensure they are able to read texts suitable for their age. When teaching vowel digraphs, follow the lesson plan above: introduce the sound, hear the sound, read and write the sound and review previously taught sounds.

You should still teach the basic high-frequency words, for example, *day* and *wait*; however, you should also teach words that are suitable for the age range. This will support children in reading age-appropriate texts. For example, *afraid, great, plain* and *sane* are words they might meet in their reading. When choosing these words, it will be helpful to look at foundation subject topics and choose words that may arise within these topics.

You will need to support children to segment these words. These sounds/words should be reviewed in short sharp bursts throughout the day to ensure they are able to read the whole word and not rely on segmenting every single word, as this will lead to stilted reading and they will struggle to comprehend what they are reading.

Working with parents and carers

It is essential that you support parents within this process. The way we teach reading now may be rather different from what parents and carers experienced as children. Adults supporting children at home will want to know how their children are learning to read. Parent meetings are a key way to ensure that parents feel confident to read with their children. If parents feel involved and understand how you are teaching their children to read, they will feel more confident reading with their children.

Model to the parents how you teach reading, showing them how to segment words and how to blend. Parents need to understand the process of decoding and encoding. Providing basic resources such as grapheme cards will support parents and carers. Training your children to explain how they share books when reading with adults will ensure that children feel confident to read alone or to read to parents and carers.

Learning outcomes review

You should now understand the features of the advanced alphabetic code and have developed an understanding of long vowel digraphs. You will now have an overview of how these phonemes can be taught in appropriate ways.

Answers to identifying long vowel phonemes activity (page 67)
The following words from the activity contain long vowel phonemes:

r<u>ai</u>n   s<u>oa</u>p   r<u>oa</u>d   b<u>ite</u>

s<u>ay</u>   wr<u>ite</u>   b<u>y</u>   t<u>ube</u>

b<u>oy</u>   sh<u>out</u>   h<u>ea</u>t   h<u>uge</u>

Answers to alternative spellings activity (page 67)
Possible spellings include: 'ee' as in *tweet*; 'ea' as in *beat*; 'ei' as in *receive*; 'ie' as in *shield*; 'e-e' as in *scene*; 'ey' as in *key*; 'y' as in *jolly*; 'i' as in *radio*; 'i-e' as in *marine*; 'e' as in *me*.

Further reading

Dombey, H (2006) Phonics and English orthography, in Lewis, M and Ellis, S (eds.) *Phonics Practice, Research and Policy.* London: Paul Chapman, pp95–104.

This chapter explores issues of the peculiarities of English spelling, which supports understanding when teaching long vowel phonemes.

Glazzard, J and Stokes, J (2013) *Teaching Synthetic Phonics and Early English.* Northwich: Critical Publishing Ltd.

See Chapter 4 for further guidance on the simple and complex alphabetic code.

Miskin, R (2011) *Read Write Inc.: Phonics Handbook.* Oxford: Oxford University Press.

This resource provides guidance on the principles and practice for Read Write Inc.

www.jollylearning.co.uk/overview-about-jolly-phonics [accessed 3 February 2015].

Provides guidance on the principles and practice of Jolly Phonics.

References

Crystal, D (2005) *The Stories of English.* London: Penguin.

Department for Education (DfE) (2013) *The National Curriculum in England: Framework Document.* London: DfE.

Jolliffe, W and Waugh, D with Carss, A (2015) *Teaching Systematic Synthetic Phonics in Primary Schools* (2nd edn.). London: SAGE.

McGuinness, D (2004) *Early Reading Instruction: What Science Really Tells Us about How to Teach Reading.* Cambridge, MA: MIT Press.

PIRLS (2011) International results in reading, in Mullis, IVS, Martin, MO, Foy, P and Drucker, KT (2012) Chestnut Hill, MA: TIMSS & PIRLS International Study Center, Boston College. Available at: **http://timssandpirls.bc.edu/pirls2011/international-results-pirls.html** [accessed 18 May 2015].

Chapter 7

Year 1: Decoding and encoding text

Teachers' Standards

Working through this chapter will help you meet the following standards:

2. Promote good progress and outcomes by pupils:

- Plan teaching to build on pupils' capabilities and prior knowledge.
- Demonstrate knowledge and understanding of how pupils learn and how this impacts on teaching.

3. Demonstrate good subject and curriculum knowledge:

- Demonstrate an understanding of and take responsibility for promoting high standards of literacy, articulacy and the correct use of standard English, whatever the teacher's specialist subject.

Links to the National Curriculum

Year 1
Pupils should be taught to:

- apply phonic knowledge and skills as the route to decode words
- respond speedily with the correct sound to graphemes (letters or groups of letters) for all 40+ phonemes, including, where applicable, alternative sounds for graphemes

- read accurately by blending sounds in unfamiliar words containing GPCs that have been taught
- read common exception words, noting unusual correspondences between spelling and sound and where these occur in the word
- read words containing taught GPCs and -s, -es, -ing, -ed, -er and -est endings
- read other words of more than one syllable that contain taught GPCs
- read aloud accurately books that are consistent with their developing phonic knowledge and that do not require them to use other strategies to work out words.

(DfE, 2013, p20)

Key focus

'Decoding' concerns the reading of symbols or letters and transferring them into sounds to make words. 'Encoding' involves spelling and is the process of turning sounds into symbols or letters. These processes are reversible and need to be taught explicitly by providing opportunities to both read and write graphemes for corresponding phonemes during phonics sessions and whenever you read and write alongside children.

How children learn to segment and blend

Blending

Blending involves looking at a written word, looking at each grapheme and using knowledge of grapheme–phoneme correspondences (GPCs) to work out which phoneme each grapheme represents and then merging these phonemes together to make a word. This is the basis of reading. Within synthetic phonics blending is the prime strategy through which words are read.

Segmenting

Segmenting involves hearing a word, splitting it up into the phonemes that make it, using knowledge of GPCs to work out which graphemes represent those phonemes, and then writing those graphemes down in the right order. This is the basis of spelling. Segmentation is the reverse of blending; it is the ability to split up a spoken word into phonemes.

It is essential that children understand the process of segmenting and blending when learning to read and write, and that these processes are reversible. Phonic programmes stress the importance of blending and segmenting once children know four GPCs. In many programmes these are s,a,t,p.

Commentary

The letters s,a,t,p provide many possibilities for creating short words such as sat, pat, tap, at, as, sap and past. Once other letters such as i and n or i and m are added, the number of possibilities increases greatly.

Activity: *s,a,t,p,i,n*

How many words can you create using the following letters only: *s,a,t,p,i,n?*

Commentary

Note that is *and as* include s, *but the* s *is sounded in the same way that we sound* z *in* zip *and* zebra. *At this stage of children's development these words might be regarded as 'tricky', since they do not have the GPC that children have learnt. Later, as they become familiar with other examples of* s *representing a* /z/ *sound (*was, has, does, *etc.), these words will no longer be 'tricky' for them.*

Tricky words (see Chapter 11)

Tricky words are those that are not phonetically plausible all the way through the word at the time when children first meet them. The National Curriculum refers to such words as *common exception words*. Children will not be able to sound out all the parts of these words. In order to teach tricky words, you will need to identify the sound that they will not be able to sound out; in Read Write Inc. (Miskin, 2011) this is called the 'Grotty Grapheme'. Once you identify this (and tell them the sound it makes within the word), you can draw children's attention to it to help them to read the word.

Remember that a word which may be called 'tricky' at one stage of children's development may cease to be tricky as their knowledge of grapheme–phoneme correspondences grows. For example, in early stages the word *was* might be read out as *wass*, because children will have learnt to sound *a* as in *ant* and *s* as in *sit*. However, they will later learn that in many words where an *a* follows a 'w' sound, the *a* is sounded in a similar way to the way we sound *o* in *cot* (*wash, want, wasp, wander*). They will also learn that *s* is often sounded in the same way as we sound *z* in *zip* (*is, as, his, does, realise*).

Each phonics programme will recommend a list of common exception/tricky words to learn and in which order (depending on the order your children learn sounds). There are non-statutory lists within the new National Curriculum framework.

Teaching tricky words in the classroom

Using mnemonics can be a helpful way for children to remember how to spell tricky words, for example: *Sally-Anne Is Dancing = said.*

Some teachers use the phrase 'looks like sounds like'. For example, when teaching *said* you might say 'it looks like *said* but sounds like *sed*'. You can then discuss the jobs the letters do in the word: *s* makes a 'sss' sound as in *snake*; *ai* makes an 'e' sound as in *bed*; and *d* makes a 'd' sound as in *dog*. So the tricky part of the word is the *ai* which makes the 'e' sound.

It can be helpful to display tricky words in the classroom. This will help support children who may know the word is tricky, but cannot remember which sound isn't phonetically regular. Some programmes promote whole learning through using flash cards, while some teachers find it helpful to have a display of these words or to provide lists of the most common words, many of which can be 'tricky', on each table when children are writing.

Activity: Identifying the tricky parts of words

Look at the common exception words below and identify the parts of the words that might prove confusing for some children in Year 1:

have   no   he   you   were   your   one

Consider if there are other words with similar spellings that might be taught alongside some of the above words; for example, *he* might be taught alongside *we, she, me* and *be*.

It is important that children can identify how many sounds are in a word. You could create a pocket chart with numbers 1–4 on and children take picture cards of simple words, for example, *on, man, dog*, and place these in the pockets which correspond to the correct number of phonemes. Once children grow in confidence, they could write words and dot/dash the phonemes. This will show you if they can clearly identify the sounds within a word and if they are using the correct graphemes when spelling, for example, *train* rather than *trayn*.

Activity: Segmenting words

How many phonemes are there in each of these words (Table 7.1)?

Table 7.1   Count the phonemes

Word	Segmented	Phonemes
train	t/r/ai/n	4
crayon		
street		
fright		
show		
start		

Case study: Making a clear distinction between reading and spelling

A Year 1 teacher, Sam, followed the programme Read Write Inc., which states that children should read 'using their eyes' (looking to identify the sounds within words) and write using their 'Fred Fingers'. This includes stamping the sounds that children hear when segmenting. When they are writing they think about the number of sounds that they should have written and use this to check they have used the correct number of graphemes.

Once children have been introduced to a sound, they read 'green words' – words children can sound out. As children blend to read these words, they identify the graphemes using dots and dashes (dot for one letter one sound, dash for two or more letters per sound). Once children have revised the letters (graphemes) allocated to a sound (phoneme), they are encouraged to read the whole word.

When children are writing the words they are encouraged to use their 'Fred Fingers', a skill that involves children looking at their non-preferred writing hand and, with the hand they write with, stamping the sounds that they can hear within the word. Children are encouraged to look at how many 'Fred Fingers'/sounds are within the word and say the sounds as they write these, and then check that they have the correct amount of sounds.

Sam found this helped to support his Year 1 class, who were preparing for the Phonics Screening Check. It also enabled children to identify which skill they were learning, and to identify that they could use these skills at other times when reading and spelling.

Using decodable texts in school

Decodable texts contain words that are at an appropriate phonic level for children to decode. Decodable texts are a supportive tool within primary schools. Some programmes are heavily rooted in such books and find them a stimulus to developing fluent reading, while others use them as a support tool to use at home. Decodable texts provide vital practice for children in reading known phonemes and blending them into words. While they should not be the only books children are exposed to, they are a good tool to encourage children to read independently and with success.

Children who read decodable texts based on their phonic ability often demonstrate an enjoyment in reading as they can read without support from adults. There are many widely available. Many schools use the stories created by Ruth Miskin used within the Read Write Inc. programme, while some schools use the popular *Biff and Chip* stories or the online stories of *Bug Club*.

Oxford Owl is a helpful website where children can use phonics books and read them online. There is a feature where children can have the book read to them or read it themselves. This is available as a website and as an app for use on tablet computers.

Main lesson

Stanley's Stick

Introduction

Read the children the book *Stanley's Stick* by John Hegley and Neal Layton. This book captures children's imagination. With a stick in hand, Stanley's options are endless – he flies to the moon, writes in the sand, goes fishing, plays a whistle and rides a dinosaur – and his imagination takes over and the magic begins. This book includes rhyme and all children will be able to participate in 'reading' the book. Once you have read the book, show the children a 'magic stick' that you have.

The lesson

On the board, display images of different uses for the magic stick, for example, *Mrs Desmond's stick is/can ... be a wand, do magic, be a fishing rod, fly*. As you show these on the board, you could add pictures of your stick being or doing these things. Show children how to segment these words, for example *w-a-n-d* (you will have to identify that this is a tricky word and that the *a* makes an 'o' sound), *f-i-sh-i-ng, r-o-d, f-l-y* (depending on the phonics stage of your children you may have introduced the fact that different graphemes make different sounds – you will need to locate this on your sound chart and discuss that the *y* is an 'igh' sound).

Take the children outside to choose their stick. Let them explore and discuss what their stick could transform into. While they are exploring their ideas, encourage them to sound out words and place their ideas on sticky notes. Collate these in the classroom and discuss what their stick could be/turn into. Explain to the children that they are going to write their own book about their stick. Model on the board how to write their sentences, discussing punctuation and how to segment words efficiently. If the children will be using tricky words that they have been taught, refer to these in the classroom and place them on the board.

When writing their own book, children should follow the model that you have shown, identifying the correct number of sounds within words and using a phonics sound chart to determine which grapheme they need to use to write the chosen sound. To write a word, children need to be able to identify how many sounds are within words. If children struggle to blend independently, you will need to assist them. This could be by supporting their ideas and giving them a phoneme frame so that they can identify the number of sounds they need. For example, Jane's stick can be a (picture of pen) _ _ _. This will ensure they can see how many sounds are in the word and will mean they are more likely to identify the correct graphemes required. The majority of Year 1 children should be able to identify how many sounds are in a word and be able to read back what they have written.

Plenary

Share children's work and discuss their ideas. Encourage children to read each other's books: can they spot any spelling mistakes? Can they support each other when segmenting words? You could then create a 'big book', using children's ideas, to keep in the book corner. Children enjoy reading books they have written and take pride in sharing books they have written.

Assessment

Look closely at children's writing to see if they are matching each phoneme with a grapheme, even if the graphemes they choose are incorrect. For example, a child may spell *stick* as 'stik', but if he or she does so this indicates that s/he is hearing all of the phonemes in the word and can provide a plausible grapheme for each. Where children are unable to match the number of phonemes to a similar number of graphemes, you may need to provide more practice in segmenting.

Commentary

Some children's spelling can appear rather random, such as when magic *is spelled as 'mjk' or* wand *as 'wdn'. You will need to work closely with children who make such errors to ensure they are hearing all the sounds all the way through words. There may be a hearing impairment which has not been detected but which needs to be addressed.*

Next lesson

When writing, always show children any tricky words they will need, support them with segmenting words, and encourage them to place the dots (single sounds) and dashes (2+ letters that make 1 sound) underneath words. This will ensure they are correctly identifying the sounds and hearing them properly. Always refer to the sound chart your school uses. If you come across a sound not on the chart (many charts only use the most common spelling graphemes), place it on the chart, identifying that it will not come up in many words, but it is useful for the children to know it.

Teaching Key Stage 2 children who may need support

Revisit the alphabetic code for gaps in their knowledge and revise blending, using the sounds children are confident with. This will ensure they are able to decode and encode independently. Revise and teach the sounds that they are unsure of to ensure they are able to read in class. Revise these sounds in short sharp bursts throughout the day. Assessment of the sounds they know and their gaps in knowledge is essential and should be done at least every half term in Key Stage 2 to ensure children are making progress.

Look closely at work in class and create word banks to support children who struggle to blend. Support them in placing dots and dashes to help them blend (and in turn segment) the words they will need. If children have previously seen a word, they are less likely to be anxious or worried by it. Identify and revise 'tricky words' that may arise in texts they are reading, so that they do not become frustrated when reading. Differentiation is key, and knowing the gaps in your children's knowledge is essential. Support children with words they will struggle to read beforehand and discuss the vocabulary they may find difficult. This will ensure that there are no surprises within the text and children should feel confident knowing the key vocabulary beforehand.

It is important to use appropriate texts. Many publishers make books that are fully decodable and designed for Key Stage 1, but they also have suitable books for Key Stage 2, which are designed like comic books to engage older children. These may be more suitable as reading books than those they read when younger and can cover topics relevant to their level of maturity, while giving them confidence when reading and, most importantly, enjoyment in reading when they do not have to segment every word.

Learning outcomes review

You should now have a clear understanding of the reversible process of decoding and encoding text. You should also understand the importance of providing opportunities for the application of phonic knowledge in reading and writing. You should be aware of the role of decodable texts within the teaching of reading.

Answers to s,a,t,p,i,n activity (page 77)

Possibilities might include: *sat, pat, tap, at, as, sap, past, pan, nap, pin, pit, tip, it, is, tan, tin, past, nit* and *nip.*

Answers to identifying tricky parts of words activity (page 78)

- *have* – if children have learnt split vowel digraphs, they will usually have found that *a-e* makes an 'ae' sound as in *gave.*

- *no* – although there are other words with a similar pattern such as *go* and *so*, children will have first learned that *o* makes an 'o' sound as in *hot*. There is the potential added confusion that *do* and *to* have different pronunciations of the *o.*

- *he* – as with *no*, there are some words like *be, me* and *she* which have the same **GPC**, but in their first encounters with *e* children will have learned that it has the sound *e* as in *bed.*

- *you* – children's first encounters with the digraph 'ou' will probably have been in words where it is sounded as *ow*, as in *about, shout* and *out.*

- *were* – when looking at the split digraph 'e-e' children will have learnt it as an 'ee' sound as in *these* and *here*. In *were* and in *where* and *there*, the *ere* is a vowel trigraph and in *were* this is sounded as an 'er' sound as in *her*, while in *there* and *where* it is sounded as an 'air' sound as in *chair.*

- *your* – children will first learn *ou* as the sound in *out, about* and *shout*. They will need to learn *your* alongside *pour* and *four*, where *our* is sounded *or* as in *for.*

- *one* – this is particularly confusing for early readers and writers, who often spell the word 'won', which is how it sounds using the **GPCs** they have learnt. The added complication that *won* is actually pronounced to rhyme with *fun* doesn't help. *Once* presents even greater problems!

Answers to segmenting words activity (page 78)

Word	Segmented	Phonemes
train	t/r/ai/n	4
crayon	c/r/ay/o/n	5
street	s/t/r/ee/t	5
fright	f/r/igh/t	4
show	sh/ow	2
start	s/t/ar/t	4

Further reading

Miskin, R (2011) *Read Write Inc.: Phonics Handbook.* Oxford: Oxford University Press.

This resource provides guidance on the principles and practice for Read Write Inc.

Waugh, D and Harrison-Palmer, R (2013) *Auditing Phonic Knowledge and Understanding.* London: SAGE.

Useful for auditing your subject knowledge for decoding and encoding and other aspects of systematic synthetic phonics.

References

Department for Education (DfE) (2013) *The National Curriculum in England: Framework Document.* London: DfE.

Hegley, J and Layton, N (2011) *Stanley's Stick.* London: Hodder Children's Books.

Read with Biff, Chip and Kipper. Oxford: Oxford University Press. Available at: **http://global.oup.com/ education/content/children/series/read-with-biff-chip-kipper** [accessed 7 April 2015].

Chapter 8

Years 1 and 2: Morphemes – prefixes, suffixes and root words

Learning outcomes

This chapter will allow you to achieve the following outcomes:

- have a clear understanding of morphemes;
- know how to teach children about adding prefixes and suffixes;
- understand compound words and how to teach them.

Teachers' Standards

Working through this chapter will help you meet the following standards:

3. Demonstrate good subject and curriculum knowledge:

- Demonstrate an understanding of and take responsibility for promoting high standards of literacy, articulacy and the correct use of standard English, whatever the teacher's specialist subject.
- If teaching early reading, demonstrate a clear understanding of systematic synthetic phonics.
- Have a secure knowledge of the relevant subject(s) and curriculum areas, foster and maintain pupils' interest in the subject, and address misunderstandings.

Links to the National Curriculum

Year 1
Pupils should be taught to:

- add prefixes and suffixes:

  o using the spelling rule for adding -s or -es as the plural marker for nouns and the third person singular marker for verbs

o using the prefix *un-*
o using *-ing, -ed, -er* and *-est* where no change is needed in the spelling of root words [for example, *helping, helped, quicker, quickest*].

(DfE, 2013, p23)

Year 2

The meaning of new words should be explained to pupils within the context of what they are reading, and they should be encouraged to use morphology (such as prefixes) to work out unknown words.

(DfE, 2013, p29)

Formation of **nouns** using **suffixes** such as *-ness, -er* and by compounding [for example, *whiteboard, superman*].

(DfE, 2013, p75)

Words, words, words

We could not possibly teach children all the words they need to know and use – there simply isn't enough time. Instead, we need to help them to understand words and how they are created. We need to help them to apply the knowledge and understanding they gain from learning about one or a few words to other words they meet.

For example, they might learn that an antonym (opposite) for *happy* can be *sad*, but can also be *unhappy*. They will learn that when we put the prefix *un-* at the beginning of a word, this means 'not'. At the same time, they might learn words like *unfriendly, unhelpful* and *untidy*. Later, when they meet words that they haven't been taught directly, they should be able to apply their knowledge to read and understand words like *unusually, unfamiliar* and *unlikely*.

An understanding of the role of morphemes is essential, as we need to know how to modify words to make plurals, adjectives, adverbs, past tenses and different parts of verbs.

What are prefixes and suffixes?

The clue is in the names. Prefixes are *morphemes* which we put before root words to modify their meaning. So the prefix *pre-* means 'before' and we can add it to words like *mature, heat* and *historic* to create *premature, preheat* and *prehistoric*. The language is always acquiring new words and prefixes are often used to create these, for example some shops advertise second-hand items as 'pre-loved'.

Suffixes are added at the ends of words to modify their meanings, for example either *-s* or *-es* is added to most English nouns to show that they are plural. We also add *-ing* to words to turn nouns like *play, jump* and *run* into verbs like *playing, jumping* and *running*.

What do prefixes and suffixes have to do with phonics?

As children's phonemic awareness develops, they begin to find common patterns in words and can read more quickly. Prefixes and suffixes have common patterns and tend to be spelled consistently. By understanding these morphemes, children can decode longer words and develop their reading comprehension skills, the ultimate aim of reading. To *et al.* (2014, p13) argue that:

> *Because many English words are morphologically related, learning one base word might increase the total vocabulary by a count of several words, if the student learns word formation processes of English. For example, if a person learns the word 'love', then morphologically-related words (i.e., loveable, lovely) can also be acquired.*

Johnston and Watson (2007, p44), too, maintain that *children's reading will become more fluent if they recognise these familiar chunks, and thus sound and blend them at the syllable level.*

What is a morpheme?

Phonemes are the smallest units of sound in words, so *dog* has three phonemes: /d/o/g/. *Morphemes* are the smallest units of meaning in words, so *love* is a single morpheme and *lovely* has two morphemes: *love* is the *root word* and *-ly* is a suffix which modifies the meaning of the root word. Similarly, *happy* is a single morpheme and *unhappy* has two morphemes: *un-* and *happy*, with the prefix *un-* modifying the meaning of the root word *happy*.

Prefixes and suffixes cannot usually stand alone as words and need to be attached to root words to give meaning, so they are known as *bound morphemes*. Morphemes that can stand alone and have meaning are called *free morphemes*. Often, in English, we put two free morphemes together to create a *compound word*, for example: *textbook, milkshake, hairbrush, handbag, football* and *timetable*.

Why do we need to teach children about morphemes?

Most English words can be modified by adding morphemes such as prefixes, suffixes and other free morphemes. If you look at the spelling appendix for Year 1 of the 2013 National Curriculum (DfE, p51), you will find that children are expected to know quite a lot about adding prefixes and suffixes to words. For example, they should be able to:

- add -*s* and -*es* to words (plural of nouns and the third person singular of verbs);

- add the endings -*ing*, -*ed* and -*er* to verbs where no change is needed to the root word;

- add -*er* and -*est* to adjectives where no change is needed to the root word.

Table 8.1, which can also be found in Chapter 11, shows the most commonly used nouns, verbs and adjectives in English. Almost all of them can be modified by adding the endings that Year 1 children need to learn. Many of those that cannot be modified in this way are irregular verbs and plurals, which are usually taught separately (see Chapter 11). The irregular noun plurals are *man – men, life – lives, child – children* and *woman – women*.

Table 8.1   The most commonly used nouns, verbs and adjectives in English

Nouns		Verbs		Adjectives	
1	time	1	be	1	good
2	person	2	have	2	new
3	year	3	do	3	first
4	way	4	say	4	last
5	day	5	get	5	long
6	thing	6	make	6	great
7	man	7	go	7	little
8	world	8	know	8	own
9	life	9	take	9	other
10	hand	10	see	10	old
11	part	11	come	11	right
12	child	12	think	12	big
13	eye	13	look	13	high
14	woman	14	want	14	different
15	place	15	give	15	small
16	work	16	use	16	large
17	week	17	find	17	next
18	case	18	tell	18	early
19	point	19	ask	19	young
20	government	20	work	20	important
21	company	21	seem	21	few
22	number	22	feel	22	public
23	group	23	try	23	bad
24	problem	24	leave	24	same
25	fact	25	call	25	able

Source: **www.oxforddictionaries.com/words/the-oec-facts-about-the-language**

Activity: Adding prefixes and suffixes

Look at the word *like* and then at some of the words we can make by using *like* as the root word and adding prefixes and suffixes:

likes, likely, alike, liken, unlike, dislike, unlikely, likeliness, likeliest, unlikeliest

Now look at the three words below and see how many words you can make using each as a root word and adding prefixes and/or suffixes:

place   pack   view

Commentary

If you chose words like placemat *and* viewpoint, *you created compound words (see below). In these words both morphemes are free and can stand alone as words. They do not have prefixes or suffixes.*

If you go on to look at Year 2's National Curriculum spelling appendix, you will find that children are expected to learn how to:

- add *-es* to nouns and verbs ending in *-y*;

- add *-ed*, *-ing*, *-er* and *-est* to a root word ending in *-y* with a consonant before it;

- add the endings *-ing*, *-ed*, *-er*, *-est* and *-y* to words ending in *-e* with a consonant before it;

- add *-ing*, *-ed*, *-er*, *-est* and *-y* to words of one syllable ending in a single consonant letter after a single vowel letter;

- recognise the suffixes *-ment*, *-ness*, *-ful*, *-less* and *-ly*.

Activity: Modifying words in National Curriculum spelling lists

By the time they reach Years 3 and 4, children have a prescribed list of 104 words that they are expected to learn to spell (Table 8.2).

Table 8.2 Year 3–4 spellings in the National Curriculum (DfE, 2013, p64)

accident	early	knowledge	purpose
actual	earth	learn	quarter
address	eight/eighth	length	question
answer	enough	library	recent
appear	exercise	material	regular
arrive	experience	medicine	reign
believe	experiment	mention	remember
bicycle	extreme	minute	sentence
breath	famous	natural	separate
breathe	favourite	naughty	special
build	February	notice	straight

(Continued)

(Continued)

busy/business	forward	occasion	strange
calendar	fruit	often	strength
caught	grammar	opposite	suppose
centre	group	ordinary	surprise
century	guard	particular	therefore
certain	guide	peculiar	though/although
circle	heard	perhaps	thought
complete	heart	popular	through
consider	height	position	various
continue	history	possess	weight
decide	imagine	possible	woman/women
describe	increase	potatoes	
different	important	pressure	
difficult	interest	probably	
disappear	island	promise	

Look at these words carefully and see which can be modified by adding prefixes and suffixes and which cannot.

Commentary

The activity above illustrates that most English words can be modified by adding prefixes and/or suffixes. It is important that children learn this because it will enable them to apply what they learn about some words to others they meet. For example, if they understand that the verb teach *becomes a noun,* teacher, *when the suffix -er is added, they will also be able to work out that someone who plays football is a* footballer, *someone who gardens is a* gardener *and so on.*

Teaching your class

This chapter includes two lessons on morphemes; one for Year 1 and one for Year 2. Each can be adapted for use with children of different abilities in the other year group.

Even before they can read, young children know a lot about adding suffixes to words. Try a simple exercise to see what they know. The Phonics Screening Test requires Year 1 children to read pseudo or invented words to check on their ability to match graphemes to phonemes. Invent some phonically regular words or use some of the ones below and draw pictures to illustrate what the words might be names for. You could try:

rutch, flid, murn, lun, pib, vatch, vuss, wob

Before showing children the words, say them and show them a picture. You might decide to make a simple drawing of each as an animal, a flower or a vehicle. As you say each word, ask the children what you would call the thing if there were two of them:

This is a *rutch*; if I had another one I'd have two …

This is a *flid*; if I had lots of them I'd have some …

Even children who cannot read will almost certainly say *rutches* for the first and *flids* for the second, because they are used to hearing those endings for plurals. They may not be able to explain that words which end with a /ch/ or /tch/ sound add -*es* in the plural, while words which end with *d* add an *s*, but because they hear plurals for *watch, match, switch,* etc. and *lid, wood, bud,* etc., they know what the endings sound like in the plural.

You can try the same thing for verbs to check their oral knowledge of verb endings in the present and past tense. Try some of these:

Make an action such as waving your arms or tapping your fingers on a table and say:

I'm *mibbing*. I'm going to do it again. What am I going to do? I'm going to …

Children will probably say *mib*.

Then say: *I did the same thing yesterday. Today I am mibbing, but yesterday I …*

Children will probably say *mibbed*.

Commentary

Of course, not all plurals are made by adding -s or -es and this leads to children and people whose first language is not English making mistakes. We often hear things like:
There were two mans *or* some sheeps, *or* I wented out *or* I swimmed, *which is quite understandable, given how often plurals are made by adding -s and past tenses by adding -ed. It is through oral work and hearing adults read to them that children become familiar with correct versions for irregular plurals and past tenses.*

The key to helping children to understand how words are modified by the addition of prefixes and suffixes is to begin with oral work. We do not suggest that you combine practising reading pseudo words with looking at prefixes and suffixes, however. It is particularly important that children develop their ability to read meaningful text with real words if they are to see reading as a useful activity.

Main lesson

Morpheme windows

In this lesson children are encouraged to think about some of the prefixes and suffixes they have learnt and to attempt some word building.

Introduction

Begin by playing some oral word games focusing on prefixes. Say a prefix such as *un-*, *pre-*, *dis-* and *re-*. Ask children to tell their neighbours as many words as they can which begin with each prefix. Write some examples on the board and discuss the words' meanings. Use the opportunity to address any misconceptions children may have. For example, some may suggest words such as *under, united* or *university* for the *un-* prefix, but *un-* does not mean 'not' in these words. Explain the meanings of the prefixes.

Commentary

Un- is one of the first prefixes children learn, but they can confuse it with *uni-, which means 'one'. If this arises, explain the difference through examples such as* united, *which means 'coming together as one'. In fact, there are very few words which begin with the* uni- *prefix and lots which begin with* un- *meaning 'not', so it will be easy to provide plenty of examples which most children will know, including* unknown, unkind, untie, undo, unload, unsafe *and* unroll. *It is a good idea to have a good quality dictionary nearby so that you can check the etymology of the words children suggest.*

Development

When you have collected some words on the board, ask children to see if they can add suffixes to any of them to modify their meaning. For example, *unlike* could become *unlikely*, *prepare* could become *prepared*, *disappoint* can become *disappointment*, *prefix* can become *prefixes* and *reset* can become *resets*.

Give children challenges to write words on paper or mini white boards, for example:

- How many words can you write beginning with *un-*?

- How many words can you write ending with *-ing*?

Word windows

To reinforce children's understanding of morphemes, you can play a simple game involving two- and three-part words that include a prefix, a root word and a suffix. Make a collection of words that have three morphemes, such as *reported, reports, unlikely, delightful* written on pieces of card which slot into a card holder with three liftable flaps. Make the card holder by sticking two pieces of card together and leaving a space in which to slot the words on cards. Number the flaps 1, 2 and 3.

Explain to children that there is a word hidden by the flaps and that they could choose any of the three to be raised to reveal part of the word. When someone has chosen a flap, lift it to reveal part of the hidden word and ask children to write down as many words as possible that might include the morpheme revealed and have three parts. For example, if *un-* was revealed under flap 1 they might write *unlucky, unlikely, unusually, unfunny*, etc. You might wish to award points for each word that is possible and write some of these correctly spelled on the board.

Next, ask someone to choose another flap to lift. If this revealed *un + fasten* you could ask them to write as many words as the hidden one could be on their white boards: these might be *unfastens, unfastened, unfastening*.

Independent work

Provide a selection of words that include the prefixes and suffixes children have been learning. Ask them to write sentences that include each one to reinforce their understanding of the morphemes. This activity is best done in pairs or threes so that children can discuss their answers. Ensure there is a dictionary for each group so that they can look the words up when necessary.

Extension

Provide children who are confident in using prefixes and suffixes with a table like the one below (Table 8.3), which has some common prefixes in the left-hand column and a series of root words in the right-hand column. Ask them to use each prefix and each root word as many times as they like to see how many words they can create. They can check that their words are correct by using a dictionary.

Table 8.3 Prefixes and root words

Prefix	Root word
un-	like
multi-	market
tri-	storey
dis-	scope
re-	use
micro-	form
mega-	store
super-	fortunate
uni-	cycle

If they create new words that can't be found in dictionaries, they could try explaining what the words might mean. For example, one group of Year 2 children made up *uncycle* and said that it meant 'walk', and *relike*, which they thought could mean 'making friends with people you'd fallen out with'.

Commentary

Many new words are formed each year by combining existing prefixes with existing words to create words which match a specific meaning. Think about unfriend, *which is used on Facebook, but which didn't exist before Facebook was introduced.*

You might go on to try similar activities with suffixes, as in the activity below.

Activity: Adding suffixes

How many new words can you create by adding suffixes to the root words? Sometimes the addition of a suffix necessitates a modification to the spelling of the root word, as in *love* and *loving, fun* and *funny* and *fit* and *fitted*. Consider how you would teach spelling generalisations for such words (Table 8.4).

Table 8.4 Root words and suffixes

Root words	Suffixes
cheer	-y
hope	-s
watch	-ful
make	-ly
fox	-es
like	-ing
help	-ed
run	-ness
fit	-less

Commentary

Activities like this help children understand how words work and how we can build them. They help them to make generalisations, which they can apply when they meet new words. For example, they will understand that words which end with -e like hope *and like usually drop the* e *when -ing is added.*

Compound words

A compound word is formed from two or more other words. For example, *bathroom* from *bath* and *room*; *football* from *foot* and *ball*. Compound words may be written in three different ways.

- As one word: *bathroom, lunchbox, hairbrush.*
- Hyphenated: *cover-up, break-in, play-off, shoot-out.*
- As two words: *bus stop, post office, rap music.*

Most compound words are nouns, but some are adjectives or verbs.

- Nouns include: *coffeetable, haircut, screwdriver*.
- Adjectives include: *risk-taking, homesick, awe-inspiring*.
- Verbs include *rubber-stamp, undertake, sunbathe*.

The words which make up a compound word must each be able to stand alone, so *peanut* is made up of *pea* and *nut*. This distinguishes compound words from those which are created by adding prefixes or suffixes to existing words, for example, *likely* is made up of *like*, which can stand alone, and the suffix *-ly*, which cannot, and *going* is made up of *go*, which can stand alone, and *-ing*, which cannot.

Lesson 2: Compound words

Introduction
Show the class some or all of the words in Table 8.5 and ask them to say them aloud with you and then with their partners.

Table 8.5 Common compound words

everyone	everybody	everything	nowhere	nobody
somewhere	anyone	anywhere	anybody	someone

Ask if anyone notices anything about the words. If necessary, prompt them by saying the words slowly with clear separation between each morpheme in each compound word: *every/one, some/where*, etc.

One way to emphasise the way in which the words are formed is to look at their antonyms or opposites; so *everyone's* opposite is *no-one* and *everybody's* opposite is *nobody*. Help children to see the roles that the different parts of the compound words play and how changing them can create words with different meanings. For example, *everyone* can become *no-one* and *someone*. You may need to explain that *no-one* is usually hyphenated or written as two separate words *(no one)* because the double *o* might lead to confusion when pronouncing the word (sometimes read in the same way as *noon*).

Extension
Ask children to find other compound words in a range of texts and show them how to separate the words into their morphemes. Get them to use dictionaries when necessary to find out their meanings.

Assessment

Note children's ability to identify words within words both when reading and writing. Can they combine words to create compounds? Are they able to find examples of compound words in texts?

Teaching Key Stage 2 children who may need support

Try giving children a selection of root words that can be combined to create compound words. In the example below (Table 8.6) many words can be used more than once to create more words, for example *headache, toothbrush, hairbrush*.

Table 8.6 Root words for combining

head	hair	brush	room
tooth	house	green	farm
school	snow	fall	water
day	class	break	ache

For children who struggle with reading and spelling, longer words such as compounds can appear daunting. However, if you explain to them that the words are actually made up of shorter, simple words this can be reassuring and can encourage them to feel more confident about spelling and reading.

Learning outcomes review

You should now have a clear understanding of morphemes and understand that words are made up of these. You should know how to teach children about adding prefixes and suffixes and understand compound words and how to teach them.

Answers to adding prefixes and suffixes activity (page 88)
How did you do? Among the possibilities are:

- place: places, placed, placing, replace, placement

- pack: unpack, repack, packs, packing, packed, package, packer

- view: views, viewing, viewer, review, preview.

Answers to modifying words in NC spelling lists activity (page 89)
In the table below you will find one example of a modification for each of the words that can be modified. In most cases, there could be several other ways to modify the words. Only *enough, perhaps, potatoes* and *therefore* cannot be modified. Note that *potatoes* is the modified (plural) version of *potato*.

accidents	earlier	knowledgeable	purposeful
actually	earthly	learner	quartered
addresses	eight/eighths	lengths	questionable
answers	enough	librarian	recently
appearance	exercises	materials	regularly
arrived	experienced	medicinal	reigned
believer	experimental	mentioned	remembered
bicycles	extremely	minutes	sentenced
breathless	famously	naturally	separates
breathing	favourites	naughtiness	specially
builder	Februaries	noticed	straighten
busy/businesses	forwards	occasionally	strangely
calendars	fruity	oftener	strengthen
uncaught	grammarian	opposites	supposed
centred	groups	ordinarily	surprised
centuries	guardian	particularly	therefore
certainty	guidance	peculiarly	although
circles	unheard	perhaps	thoughtful
completed	hearten	popularity	throughout
considered	heights	positioned	variously
continued	historical	possession	weighty
decider	imaginative	possibility	womanly
describes	increased	potatoes	
differently	importantly	pressurize	
difficulty	interested	improbably	
disappearance	islands	promised	

Answers to adding suffixes activity (page 94)

You probably managed to create several words with the same suffix, as well as several with the same roots. Possible words include:

- cheer: cheery, cheerful, cheers, cheering, cheered

- hope: hopes, hopeful, hoped, hopeless, hoping

- watch: watches, watchful, watching, watched

- make: makes, making, maker

- fox: foxy, foxes, foxing, foxed

- like: likes, likely, likes, liking, likeness

- help: helps, helpful, helped, helping, helpless

- run: runny, runs, running

- fit: fits, fitful, fitting, fitted, fitness

References

Department for Education (DfE) (2013) *The National Curriculum in England: Framework Document*. London: DfE.

Johnston, R and Watson, J (2007) *Teaching Synthetic Phonics*. Exeter: Learning Matters.

Jolliffe, W and Waugh, D with Carss, A (2015) *Teaching Systematic Synthetic Phonics in Primary Schools*. London: SAGE.

A useful resource for developing your understanding of morphology; see especially Chapter 6.

Oxford Dictionaries website. Available at: **www.oxforddictionaries.com/words/the-oec-facts-about-the-language** [accessed 6 April 2015].

To, N, Tighe, E and Binder, K (2014) Investigating morphological awareness and the processing of transparent and opaque words in adults with low literacy skills and in skilled readers. *Journal of Research in Reading*, 14 (2): 1–18.

Waugh, D, Warner, C and Waugh, R (2013) *Teaching Grammar, Punctuation and Spelling in Primary Schools*. London: SAGE, especially Chapters 2 and 3.

Waugh, D, Allott, K, Waugh, R, English, E and Bulmer, E (2014) *The Spelling, Punctuation and Grammar App*. Morecambe: Children Count Ltd. (available through the App Store).

Chapter 9

Year 2: Homophones and contractions

Learning outcomes

This chapter will allow you to achieve the following outcomes:

- understand homophones and contractions;
- explore ways in which homophones and contractions can be taught;
- identify useful resources that can be used to support spelling.

Teachers' Standards

Working through this chapter will help you meet the following standards:

2. Promote good progress and outcomes by pupils:

- Be accountable for pupils' attainment, progress and outcomes.
- Be aware of pupils' capabilities and their prior knowledge, and plan teaching to build on these.

3. Demonstrate good subject and curriculum knowledge:

- Demonstrate an understanding of and take responsibility for promoting high standards of literacy, articulacy and the correct use of standard English, whatever the teacher's specialist subject.

Links to the National Curriculum

Homophones and contractions are a feature of the National Curriculum at Key Stage 1 and beyond.

Key Stage 1 statutory requirement

Year 1

Pupils should be taught to:

- read words with contractions [for example, *I'm*, *I'll*, *we'll*], and understand that the apostrophe represents the omitted letter(s).

(DfE, 2013, p20)

Year 2

Pupils should be taught to:

- learn new ways of spelling phonemes for which one or more spellings are already known, and learn some words with each spelling, including a few common homophones
- distinguish between homophones and near-homophones.

(DfE, 2013, p29)

Before reading this chapter, try the activity below:

Activity: Homophones

What do these words have in common?

there	sea	two	buy	maid	thyme
sew	knot	four	know	sore	hear

What is a homophone?

Homophones are words which sound the same as each other, but are spelled differently and have different meanings, for example, *wait* and *weight*, *father* and *farther*, *chews* and *choose*. The word homophone means 'same sound', with *homo* meaning 'same' and *phone* relating to sound. English has lots of homophones and they can cause confusion when writers select the wrong word. They are often the basis of children's jokes, such as:

What's black and white and red all over?

– A newspaper! (black and white and *read* all over).

Once children are secure in their basic phonic knowledge, they should begin to notice patterns and different spellings within words. Exploring these and discussing what children can see will allow you to make judgements about their phonic knowledge and their understanding of vocabulary. Children may notice homophones and may identify that the words have different spellings. However, you will need to teach these explicitly. Although there is no statutory word list of homophones within the National Curriculum, there are non-statutory examples.

Clearly, when children are reading these words they use the context of the sentence and text to identify meaning – the fact that the word is a homophone does not impact on reading if children are taught to continuously self-monitor their reading, checking what they have read makes sense. Children should be encouraged to ask questions and to comment as they read, and it is useful for the teacher to model this 'thinking aloud', demonstrating how the teacher notices possible alternative meanings and modelling and why one word meaning is disregarded in the context of the sentence.

What is a near-homophone?

Near-homophones are pairs of words which almost sound the same and sometimes do sound the same when one is mispronounced or not pronounced clearly, for example: *prince* and *prints*, *affect* and *effect*, *guest* and *guessed*, *one* and *won*. Some words become homophones or near-homophones in some accents but not in others. For example, *are* and *our* have very similar pronunciations in many areas of England.

How common are homophones?

There are lots of homophones in English. Table 9.1 shows some of the common English homophones and near-homophones that children may meet in Key Stages 1 and 2.

Table 9.1 Homophones

air, heir	heard, herd	ring, wring
aisle, I'll, isle	hi, high	road, rode
allowed, aloud	higher, hire	roe, row
aren't, aunt	him, hymn	role, roll
ate, eight	hoarse, horse	root, route
awe, oar, or, ore	holy, wholly	rose, rows
aye, eye, I	hour, our	rouse, rows
bail, bale	in, inn	sale, sail
ball, bawl	it's, its	sauce, source
band, banned	jewel, joule	saw, soar, sore
bare, bear	key, quay	scene, seen
be, bee	knave, nave	sea, see
beach, beech	knead, need	seam, seem
bean, been	knew, new	seas, sees, seize
beat, beet	knight, night	sew, so, sow
berry, bury	knit, nit	shoe, shoo
blew, blue	knock, nock	side, sighed
boar, bore	knot, not	slay, sleigh
board, bored	know, no	some, sum
boarder, border	knows, nose	son, sun
bold, bowled	laps, lapse	sort, sought
bough, bow	larva, lava	stair, stare
boy, buoy	lead, led	stake, steak

(Continued)

Table 9.1 (Continued)

brake, break	leak, leek	stalk, stork
bread, bred	lessen, lesson	stationary, stationery
buy, by	loan, lone	steal, steel
caught, court	made, maid	stile, style
ceiling, sealing	mail, male	storey, story
cell, sell	main, mane	sweet, suite
cent, scent, sent	mare, mayor	tacks, tax
cereal, serial	meat, meet, mete	tale, tail
cheap, cheep	medal, meddle	tea, tee
check, cheque	meter, metre	team, teem
cite, sight, site	miner, minor	teas, tease
coarse, course	mind, mined	there, their, they're
currant, current	missed, mist	threw, through
days, daze	mode, mowed	throne, thrown
dear, deer	moor, more	thyme, time
dew, due	moose, mousse	tide, tied
die, dye	morning, mourning	tire, tyre
draft, draught	muscle, mussel	to, too, two
dual, duel	naval, navel	toad, toed, towed
earn, urn	nay, neigh	told, tolled
ewe, yew, you	oh, owe	vain, vane, vein
fair, fare	one, won	vale, veil
farther, father	packed, pact	wail, wale, whale
faun, fawn	pail, pale	waist, waste
feat, feet	pain, pane	wait, weight
few, phew	pair, pare, pear	waive, wave
find, fined	pause, paws, pours	war, wore
fir, fur	pea, pee	ware, wear, where
flaw, floor	peace, piece	warn, worn
flea, flee	peal, peel	watt, what
flour, flower	peer, pier	wax, whacks
for, fore, four	place, plaice	way, weigh, whey
fort, fought	plain, plane	we, wee
forth, fourth	pleas, please	weak, week
foul, fowl	pole, poll	we'd, weed
freeze, frieze	practice, practise	weal, we'll, wheel
genes, jeans	praise, prays, preys	weather, whether
gnaw, nor	principal, principle	weir, we're
grate, great	rain, reign, rein	were, whirr
groan, grown	raise, rays	which, witch
guessed, guest	rap, wrap	whine, wine
hail, hale	raw, roar	whirled, world
hair, hare	read, reed	who's, whose
hay, hey	read, red	wood, would
heal, heel, he'll	real, reel	yore, your, you're
hear, here	right, write	

How should we teach homophones?

There is some debate as to the best way to teach homophones. Often, homophones are taught together, and different word meanings are explained. For example, *there, their* and *they're* are often taught together and teachers explain their different meanings. However, some researchers (for example, Mudd, 1994) maintain that learning in this way can actually cause confusion. Mudd (1994) suggested that grouping homophones together for teaching worked well for good spellers (who were likely already to know the different spellings) but not for weaker spellers.

The Schonell spelling lists, which were for many years the source for spelling lists for teachers, grouped words that were visually similar and Schonell recommended that homophones should be taught separately. Thus, *there* would be taught alongside *here* and *where*, and *they're* might be taught with other contractions such as *we're* and *you're*. It is interesting that *their* is so often taught alongside *there*, since the spelling pattern 'eir' is rarely found in other words. Among the few such words are *heir, weir, weird*, two of which (*heir* and *weir*) are rarely used by children in their writing, However, *weird*, which is often spelled incorrectly as 'wierd', is a word children do use, and linking it to *their* could be helpful, even though 'eir' is pronounced differently in each word.

Crystal (2012) maintains that words should be taught in a meaningful context, especially where they might be confused. He argues that when homophones are taught together, this invites confusion, even when it did not previously exist. You will need to decide when it might be appropriate to teach homophones together and when this should be avoided because to do so may cause confusion. In this chapter, we have included a lesson plan that includes homophones being taught together, but you may wish to consider alternative approaches too.

Homographs and homonyms

It is important not to confuse homophones with homonyms and homographs.

Homographs are words that are spelled the same but which sound different (from *homo* meaning 'same' and *graph* relating to writing). Think of *wound* (an injury) and *wound* (the past tense of *wind*), *wind the clock* and *the wind which blows*, *record a programme* and *break a record*.

Homonyms are pairs of words with different meanings, and often different origins, but which sound and are spelled the same.

Activity: Homonyms

Look at the words below, all of which are homonyms, and think about the different meanings they can have.

bear, bat, bark, bank, can, down, fine, fair, light, park, rock, rose, saw, quarry

Homonyms do not present the same problems for spellings as homophones, because their spellings are consistent whatever the meaning of the words, although they do have the potential to confuse readers if they are not focusing on meaning as they read. In the same way as the 'think aloud' approach was described above, this approach is useful to ensure that children are not merely decoding but are reading for meaning.

Teaching your class: Linking homophones and phonic knowledge

Begin by displaying pairs of homophones randomly on a board. You might make cards and use magnetic holders; you could simply write the words; or you could create a display using the interactive white board where the words can be dragged across the screen. Ask children to spot and match the pairs of words. You might use some of the following words (Table 9.2).

Table 9.2 Spot the pairs

sun	son	way	weight
hare	hair	eight	ate
hole	whole	mail	male
write	right	flower	flour
bored	board	groan	grown
eye	I	hear	here

Once children have identified homophones (for example, *hare* and *hair*), encourage them to look closely at the spellings. Is there a way that they can remember which graphemes to use to write the words correctly? Looking closely at the parts of pairs of homophones that differ will remind children of the possible ways they can write that particular sound. It is essential here to refer back to the meanings of the words as this gives children another hook to support their memory of how to spell the words.

When introducing homophones, for example, *night* and *knight*, discuss the spellings. If children know both words have the same /ie/ sound represented by 'igh', they should be able to identify that the changes in spelling occur within the *n* sound. This links directly to the National Curriculum objectives set out for Year 2 spelling: *the N sound spelled kn and (less often) gn at the beginning of words* (DfE, 2013). Encourage children to look at spelling charts you have in the classroom (or ones you have made). Can they make predictions about how the words will be spelled? You will be able to assess a lot about their phonic knowledge from these discussions and understand where their gaps in phonic knowledge may be.

Main lesson

Teaching homophones

Introduction

Revisit homophones and discuss what the word means. Are there any other words that they know that sound the same but have different meanings? Can they think of any words that they have discussed during phonics lessons?

At this stage you may wish to do some sentence work, either as shared writing or in pairs or independently, so that children see the words used in sentences.

Explain that you will be reading the book called *Dear Deer* (*A Book of Homophones*, 2010 by Gene Barretta). What do they notice about the title? Can they make any predictions about the book from the front cover? Discuss the meaning of the words *dear* and *deer*. Discuss why they are homophones and look at your sound chart to identify the different ways of spelling the 'ear' sound.

In the story, Aunt Ant is writing to her nephew about her new neighbours at the zoo. She writes about the *moose who loves mousse* and *ate eight bowls*; and *the whale that was prone to wail*, etc. Encourage children to listen for homophones while you read the story. You may need to discuss some of the different meanings of words; for example, children may not know meanings for *the whale that wails*. Encourage children to put actions to these words; this will help support their understanding of the meaning. Once you have read the story, read it again, encouraging children to perform an action (for example, put up their thumbs) when they hear a homophone.

Using the homophones from the book, ask children to play snap, taking it in turns to turn over cards to match homophones. Once they have been able to match the homophones, encourage them to identify the different ways of spelling the words. Ask them to look closely at the graphemes that make the same sound, e.g. *whale* and *wail*; children should identify different spellings for *w* being 'w' and 'wh'. They should also notice that the 'ae' sound is spelled 'ai' and 'a-e' within these words.

Development

Once children have discussed the homophones, ask them to put these words into 'sentences', for example, for *ate/eight*:

The greedy cat *ate eight* enormous fish.

Ask children to say these sentences to their partners. Can they improve them? Could they add adjectives to the sentences? If you do this, children need to have a purpose to the sentence improvement – remember that a sentence isn't always improved by adding an adjective.

Display homophones on the board so that the children are not restricted to the ones in the book. Include *there/their/they're, here/hear, see/sea, bare/bear, sun/son, to/too/two, be/bee, blue/blew, night/knight*. Once children have decided on their sentence, they can create their own page of a class big book, writing their sentence and illustrating their page. When you have put these pages together, share your class book of homophones.

Extension

Give children a selection of homophones and near-homophones from Table 9.1 and ask them to use dictionaries to find what any unfamiliar words mean and to use these in sentences orally and then in writing.

Assessment

To check if children have understood common spellings for the phonemes in the words they have used in the lesson, ask them to spell some other words which have not been discussed but which include similar spelling patterns, for example: *bright, wear, chew, cue, near, tea*. Do they make phonically plausible attempts at spelling the words? Are the spelling patterns presented in the correct order?

Teaching Key Stage 2 children who may need support

Provide children with a selection of homophones and ask them to find examples in their reading books and in other texts. Give them sentences with alternative words needed for completion, for example: 'I am going *to/too/two* London'. Encourage them to work in pairs and discuss their choices.

There are many games and activities available online, including one from the BBC's adult Skillswise website, which is interactive: **www.bbc.co.uk/skillswise/game/ en21watc-game-paris-word**.

It is important to discuss the meaning and put these words into sentences to ensure children understand that even though the words sound the same they have two different meanings.

As children develop their understanding of homophones, they will find examples of contractions which have the same sound as other words, for example: *we're* and *weir; they're* and *there; we'll* and *wheel; I'll, aisle* and *isle*. There can be confusion when they first encounter words that have apostrophes within them and sometimes this leads to some rather peculiar spellings!

Contractions

When we speak and when we write in an informal way or when we write dialogue, we often use contractions. Apostrophes are used to mark omission (something is missing), as for example in the contractions *can't, haven't, wouldn't, who's*, where the apostrophe is used in place of the missing letters. For example:

I *can't* play the piano. (*can't* is used instead of *cannot*)

She *shouldn't* play football there. (*shouldn't* is used instead of *should not*)

Most contractions are quite easy to understand because the apostrophe replaces a single letter. However, some are more complex, with the apostrophe replacing two or more letters as in *won't, shan't* and *you'd*. *Won't* is particularly challenging, given that *will not* changes to *won't* and the vowel changes from *i* to *o*, as well as the letters *ll* and *o* being omitted. And *shan't* has letters missing in two places, but we usually only put an apostrophe in to show that the *o* is missing from *shall not*, although in nineteenth century texts *shan't* was often written as 'sha'n't'.

Table 9.3 shows a range of contractions with their full form and the missing letters that are replaced by an apostrophe. You may wish to create something similar for your classroom.

Table 9.3 Common contractions

Words in full	Contracted form	Missing letters
let us	let's	u
should not	shouldn't	o
could not	couldn't	o
do not	don't	o
we are	we're	a
I am	I'm	a
you are	you're	a
it is	it's	i
that is	that's	i

Commentary

Children often begin to notice apostrophes in Year 1 and this can lead to an outbreak of apostrophes in words which don't need them, including plurals, where the 'greengrocer's apostrophe' often seems to appear before every s. Such apostrophes are often referred to as 'greengrocers' apostrophes' because they are often seen on fruit and vegetable market stalls (Truss, 2003). Because the plural form of most nouns used in English sounds, when spoken aloud, like the possessive form (for example, the banana's skin *and* a bunch of bananas), *people sometimes put an apostrophe in both versions. This is another example of homophones causing confusion! It is thought that the term 'greengrocers' apostrophes' was coined in the mid-twentieth century by a teacher in Liverpool, England.*

Activity: A common mistake

One of the most common mistakes children and some adults make is to say and sometimes write *could of*, *should of* and *would of* rather than *could have/could've*, *should have/should've* and *would have/would've*. Why do you think they make this mistake?

Lesson: Teaching contractions

Introduce the book *I'm and Won't, They're and Don't: What's a Contraction?* by Brian P. Cleary. This book uses rhymes to teach contractions, and children enjoy looking for them within this book. This book supports all abilities with the contractions printed in colour.

Once children have listened to the rhymes in the book, discuss what a contraction is and how you would use it. Explain that a contraction identifies missing letter(s). Once children understand what a contraction is, read the book again, this time giving the children sticky notes. When they hear a contraction, ask them to write it down. Ask them to work with their partners and discuss which words the contraction is made from, for example: *they're – they are*. Ask children to discuss with their partners how to put these contractions into sentences, and then get them to share these with others.

Development
Making pairs: this activity will consolidate children's learning. Find matching gloves, shoes or buckets and spades. Children write the two words on one shoe and then on the matching shoe write the word as a contraction with the apostrophe, for example: *have not* would be on one shoe and *haven't* on the other. They then ask others to make matching pairs.

Extension
Give children a selection of contractions and ask them to sort them into '*have*, *has* and *had* contractions'; '*am*, *is* and *are* contractions'; '*not* contractions'; and '*would* and *will* contractions'. For example:

Have, *has* and *had* contractions: *I've, you've, we've, they've*

Am, *is* and *are* contractions: *I'm, you're, he's, she's, it's, we're, they're, that's, who's*

Not contractions: *aren't, can't, couldn't, didn't, doesn't, don't, hasn't, haven't, isn't, shouldn't, wasn't, weren't, won't, wouldn't*

Would and *will* contractions: *I'll, you'll, he'll, she'll, it'll, we'll, they'll, that'll, who'll, I'd, you'd, he'd, she'd, it'd, we'd, they'd, that'd*

Commentary

Children often misplace apostrophes in contractions because they have not understood that an apostrophe replaces missing letters. You will find examples like: do'nt, would'nt *and* did'nt. *Whenever these arise, it is important to explain by getting children to say the fuller version, writing it down and then asking them to say which letters are missed out in the contracted version. Make it clear that the apostrophe shows where the missing letters would have been.*

Further extension activities

- Identifying contractions in written text: place an extract from a story you have read on the board (ensure there are examples of contractions) and ask children to identify the contractions and what they would be without the contraction.

- Playing card game pairs: make a set of cards that includes pairs of two words and their contractions. For example, *did not* and *didn't*. Children turn over the cards and try to make a pair.

The *Jumpstart Grammar* text by Pie Corbett and Julia Strong (2014) has a range of suggested games and activities to support understanding about the use of the apostrophe. There is also useful guidance on the Talk for Writing website.

Teaching Key Stage 2 children who may need support

Besides revisiting the contractions taught at Key Stage 1, children could look at contractions of place names. These can be found on road signs (B'ham, B'pool, L'pool, N'castle) and road surfaces and are used so that they take up less space than the full versions. Make use of examples from signs and from football league tables (T'ham, Nott'm, B'burn) to discuss with children the reason for using apostrophes in such abbreviations and to highlight that the apostrophes indicate that letters are missing.

Learning outcomes review

You should now have a good understanding of homophones and contractions and know of ways in which homophones and contractions can be taught. You should be able to address children's misconceptions and plan effective interactive lessons to develop their subject knowledge.

You will also be aware of a range of useful resources that can be used to support your teaching and children's learning.

Answers to homophones activity (page 100)
Each word has a homophone that is one of the 100 most common words in English:

- there – their, sea – see, two – too, buy – by, maid – made, thyme – time

- sew – so, knot – not, four – for, know – no, sore – saw, hear – here.

Answers to homonyms activity (page 103)
You were asked to look at a list of homonyms and think about the different meanings they can have. Possible answers are as follows.

- *Bear* can be an animal or be used to mean 'carry' or 'tolerate'.

- *Bat* can be an animal or a verb 'to hit' (to bat away) or an implement for hitting, as in a cricket bat.

- *Bark* can be part of a tree or a noise made by a dog or the act of making that noise.

- *Bank* can be the side of a river, a place where money or supplies are kept or a verb 'to slope or turn at an angle'.

- *Can* may be a tin or part of the verb 'to be able'.

- *Down* can be a preposition or the fluff of young birds.

- *Fine* can be an adjective or a charge imposed for breaking rules.

- *Fair* can be an adjective meaning 'light in colour' or meaning 'equitable' or 'just', or a gathering for selling things.

- *Light* can be an adjective or an illumination.

- *Park* can be a place for recreation or a verb meaning 'to put something somewhere'.

- *Rock* can be stone or a verb 'to move to and fro', or a type of music.

- *Rose* can be the past tense of the verb 'to rise' or a flower.

- *Saw* can be a tool or the past tense of 'to see'.

- *Quarry* can be an excavation or something that is being pursued.

Answers to common mistake activity (page 108)
When we speak we shorten some words and introduce contractions. The *'ve* at the end of *should've, would've* and *could've* sounds the same as *of* when we say things like *a bag of chips* or *a packet of sweets*. Children therefore assume that the final part of the words is *of* rather than the *'ve* abbreviation of *have*. *Have* is a verb and *of* is clearly not, and so *could of, should of* and *would of* are grammatically incorrect.

Further reading

Resource for homophones
'A Misspelled Tail' by Elizabeth T. Corbett, which originally appeared in the children's magazine *St. Nicholas* (1893), may give you ideas for writing your own homophone poems. Some of the vocabulary and idioms may be challenging for twenty-first century children, but some might look at the poem as an extension activity and could use dictionaries to find out the meanings of some of the unfamiliar vocabulary.

> A little buoy said: "Mother, deer,
> May I go out too play?
> The son is bright, the heir is clear;
> Owe, mother, don't say neigh!"
>
> "Go fourth, my sun," the mother said.
> The ant said, "Take ewer slay,
> Your gneiss knew sled awl painted read,
> But dew not lose your weigh."
>
> "Ah, know," he cried, and sought the street
> With hart sew full of glee—
> The weather changed—and snow and sleet
> And reign, fell steadily.
>
> Threw snowdrifts grate, threw watery pool,
> He flue with mite and mane—

Said he, "Though I wood walk by rule,
I am not rite, 't is plane."

"I'd like to meat sum kindly sole,
For hear gnu dangers weight,
And yonder stairs a treacherous whole—
Two sloe has been my gate.

"A peace of bred, a nice hot stake,
I'd chews if I were home,
This crewel fete my hart will brake,
Eye love knot thus to roam.

"I'm week and pail, I've mist my rode,"
But here a carte came past,
He and his sled were safely toad
Back two his home at last.

Source: **http://grammar.about.com/od/spelling/a/A-Misspelled-Tail-By-Elizabeth-T-Corbett.htm**

Books that use homophones

How Much Can a Bare Bear Bear? What Are Homonyms and Homophones? (Words Are CATegorical) by Brian P. Cleary (2007; paperback). This book uses some American spelling, but it is useful as an additional reference book or for children to read in the library.

The King Who Rained by Fred Gwynne (1987; New York: Aladdin Books). The illustrations show a bewildered young girl who gets tripped up over homophones. It is a story children will love to read and they will enjoy looking for homophones.

A Chocolate Moose for Dinner by Fred Gwynne (1976; New York: Aladdin Books). This book is written by the same author as *The King Who Rained*. Children may struggle to understand the homophones as they are difficult, e.g. Mum says there are aeroplane hangers (shows a picture of aeroplanes on coat hangers). Some of the phrases are American and children may struggle to understand the concept, for example the book references comparisons to a *carpool*.

Eight Ate: A Feast of Homonym Riddles by Marvin Terban and G. Maestro (2007; New York: Clarion). A wealth of clever riddles makes this classic book by Marvin Terban a great resource for teaching multiple meaning words. Children may find some of the vocabulary tricky, for example: *foul, fowl*. It may need to be shared with an adult to fully appreciate the riddles.

A Dictionary of Homophones by Leslie Presson (1997; paperback). This is in the format of a dictionary, but uses colours and pictures to make it interesting for children. This would make a useful addition to a class library.

Story books that use contractions

Once children can identify contractions, it is important that they can identify these within written texts. Children will enjoy looking for them in books and talking about what they mean. These books are useful when reading and looking for contractions or teaching contractions.

Don't Let the Pigeon Drive the Bus by Mo Willems.

If You Give a Mouse a Cookie by Laura Joffe Numeroff; illustrated by Felicia Bond.

"I Can't" Said the Ant by Polly Cameron (author, illustrator) (paperback).

If You Were a Contraction (Word Fun) by Trisha Shasken; illustrated by Sara Gray.

Greedy Apostrophe: A Cautionary Tale by Jan Carr; illustrated by Ethan Long.

If You Were an Apostrophe (Word Fun) by Shelly Lyons; illustrated by Sara Gray.

Alfie the Apostrophe by Moira Rose Donohue; illustrated by Joann Adinolfi.

References

Barretta, G (2010) *Dear Deer: A Book of Homophones.* New York: Square Fish Paperbacks.

Cleary, B (2012) *I'm and Won't, They're and Don't: What's a Contraction?* Minneapolis: Millbrook Press.

Corbett, P and Strong, J (2014) *Jumpstart! Grammar: Games and Activities for Ages 6–14.* London: David Fulton.

Crystal, D (2012) *Spell It Out: The Singular Story of English Spelling.* London: Profile Books.

Department for Education (DfE) (2013) *The National Curriculum in England: Framework Document.* London: DfE.

Mudd, N (1994) *Effective Spelling: A Practical Guide for Teachers.* London: Hodder and Stoughton.

Talk for Writing website. Available at: **http://www.talk4writing.co.uk**

Truss, L (2003) *Eats, Shoots & Leaves: The Zero Tolerance Approach to Punctuation.* London: Profile Books.

Chapter 10

Year 2: Phonics into spelling

Learning outcomes

This chapter will allow you to achieve the following outcomes:

- have a clear understanding of how to build upon children's phonic knowledge to support their spelling;
- identify how we use phonics to support spelling;
- be aware of strategies to teach spelling patterns.

Teachers' Standards

Working through this chapter will help you meet the following standards:

3. Demonstrate good subject and curriculum knowledge:

- Demonstrate an understanding of and take responsibility for promoting high standards of literacy, articulacy and the correct use of standard English, whatever the teacher's specialist subject.
- If teaching early reading, demonstrate a clear understanding of systematic synthetic phonics.
- Have a secure knowledge of the relevant subject(s) and curriculum areas, foster and maintain pupils' interest in the subject, and address misunderstandings.

Links to the National Curriculum

Year 2
They should be able to spell correctly many of the words covered in year 1 (see English Appendix 1). They should also be able to make phonically plausible attempts to spell words they have not yet learnt.

It is important to recognise that pupils begin to meet extra challenges in terms of spelling during Year 2. Increasingly, they should learn that there is not always an obvious connection between the way a word is said and the way it is spelt. Variations include different ways of spelling the same sound, the use of so-called silent letters and groups of letters in some words and, sometimes, spelling that has become separated from the way that words are now pronounced, such as the 'le' ending in table.

(DfE, 2013, p26)

Pupils should be taught to spell by:

- segmenting spoken words into phonemes and representing these by graphemes, spelling many correctly;
- learning new ways of spelling phonemes for which one or more spellings are already known, and learn some words with each spelling, including a few common homophones;
- learning to spell common exception words;
- learning to spell more words with contracted forms;
- learning the possessive apostrophe (singular) [for example, the girl's book];
- distinguishing between homophones and near-homophones;
- adding suffixes to spell longer words, including -ment, -ness, -ful, -les;
- applying spelling rules and guidance, as listed in English Appendix 1.

(DfE, 2013, p29)

This chapter builds on the work done in Chapter 8 on morphemes – prefixes, suffixes and root words. Spelling is a key element of the National Curriculum and can, given the inconsistencies in grapheme–phoneme correspondences in English, be challenging for both children and teachers.

As children develop confidence in recognising the graphemes most commonly used to represent the 44 speech sounds, they are ready to investigate spelling patterns in more depth. This stage is important because it ensures that children's writing progresses from being phonetically plausible, but perhaps misspelled, to following standard English spelling. For example, in their early attempts at writing children might spell *house* as 'howse', *when* as 'wen', *because* as 'becos' and *school* as 'skool'. The next stage is to develop greater accuracy and a knowledge that phonemes can be represented by many different graphemes.

How do schools teach spelling?

Spelling can be taught in many different ways and there are different strategies for teaching different types of word. Some schools use spelling schemes and there are many available. Read Write Inc. progresses from a phonic programme to a spelling programme which is matched to the National Curriculum. It is taught in whole year groups (once children have finished the phonics programme) and has modules that teach spelling patterns. Nelson English Skills is another popular support tool in which children have workbooks and practice books. This programme has planned progression matching the National Curriculum and has activities, including comprehension, spelling and grammar.

Many schools make use of Support for Spelling (DCSF, 2009), which is a progression from Letters and Sounds (DfES, 2007). This resource provides lesson plans and lots of examples for each of the spelling generalisations taught. Although aimed particularly at Key Stage 2, it is also useful for higher attaining Year 2 children, as well as as a resource when planning for any primary age group.

Teaching your class

Children can learn to spell through lots of different resources and activities. Your school may follow a programme or you may be able to construct your own way of teaching children to spell, drawing upon a range of resources. The activities below can be done throughout the day and as revision, if your school does follow a particular programme, or as a supplement to work from a programme.

Strategies for learning and revision

Introducing the pattern/rule

Identifying clearly what children will be learning allows them to spot patterns and make judgements/predictions for themselves. For example, they might look at words with suffixes and be shown how the root word is sometimes modified when a suffix is added, as in *happy* and *happily*, and *lovely* and *loveliness*.

Identifying sounds within the word

Show children the words they will be using and encourage them to identify the sounds within the words by placing a dot underneath the single sounds and a dash for sounds with two letters or more.

b oo k

This reinforces their phonic knowledge and allows them to see the impact a spelling rule may have. For example, *run – running*: children will need to be able to identify that the grapheme before *-ing* has doubled, but still makes the same sound. This can lead to spelling investigations.

Spelling investigations

Some people question the value of teaching spelling rules, citing the flawed 'i before e except after c' rule, which has so many exceptions that it is of little use (think of *their, rein, science, being, seeing, foreign, forfeit, freight, heifer, height, heinous, heir, heist, neigh, neighbour, neither*, etc.). However, there are many rules and generalisations that are worth learning because they are more consistent and have few exceptions.

Children will understand and remember these if they are given opportunities to research them and work out the generalisations for themselves. This also provides you with opportunities to note and then address their misconceptions. For the example above of words gaining the *-ing* suffix, children could be asked to look at collections of common words which have *-ing* endings and see if they can work out what happens to the root words when *-ing* is added. You could try this with words like:

come – coming

hit – hitting

run – running

like – liking

bat – batting

wet – wetting

sit – sitting

hope – hoping

hop – hopping

Can children work out when the consonant before *-ing* is doubled and what happens to words which end with *e* when *-ing* is added? There are exceptions to this 'rule' (e.g. *benefit – benefiting*), but these are rare and unlikely to be met by most Key Stage 1 children.

Other spelling investigations could include:

• finding out which letters English words do not end with (*v, j* and *q*);

• finding out which letter always follows *q* in English words (*u*);

• working out a rule for making nouns which end with *y* into plurals (e.g. *baby – babies, lady – ladies, monkey – monkeys, boy – boys, key – keys*).

Activity: Making words which end with *y* into plurals

Can you work out a rule or generalisation for making words that end with *y* into plurals? When you feel confident you have done this, test your hypothesis by looking at lots of words that end with *y* and their plurals (see end of chapter for a solution).

Identifying the correct spelling

Try providing children with sentences or a paragraph using the spelling rule or generalisation recently learnt, and encourage them to find words that follow the rule. Children should write out the words (taking care to copy the correct spelling) and put them into their own sentences. Ask them to read each other's sentences and check they have used the correct spelling.

Putting the word into context

Place sentences on the board with the focus word having two spellings, for example, 'I love running/runing in the rain'. Children choose the correct spelling and explain to their partners why they have chosen this spelling. This allows the teacher to assess who has understood the spelling focus and helps to identify those who may need more support. Hearing children's explanations and sharing their thoughts with a partner also allows you to discover if they have understood and identified the pattern they can see occurring.

Informal spelling tests

After looking at the words/pattern for a whole week, children should be able to write these words independently. Spelling tests do not have to be conducted in the traditional sense; the children do not necessarily have to take a list home and learn words. After looking at the words throughout the week, the children should be able to recall the words. They can test each other on the words they have read during the week. They should mark each other's work and discuss if they think there are any mistakes. It is important to provide them with the correct answers so that they can check their work. They can then help each other to learn the words that they spelled incorrectly.

Main lesson

Adding the suffix -y

Introducing the pattern/rule

While exploring phonics children may have noticed the 'ea' sound is spelled '-y' when placed as a suffix (for example, *laze – lazy, run – runny, love – lovely*) or when it ends a word (for example, *baby, lady, any, many*). You will need to explain to the children that a suffix is a letter (or group of letters) that when added to the end of a word modifies its meaning. Display some words that can be used with the suffix -*y* and discuss how the word changes, for example: *sleep – sleepy, run – runny, fun – funny*. Encourage children to say these words in sentences so that they can clearly hear how the meaning of the word changes. For example, *I go to sleep at night and I feel very sleepy because I did not go to bed early*.

> **Commentary**
>
> *Adding* -y *turns nouns like* snow *into adjectives* (snowy) *that mean having or like something; adding* -ly *changes adjectives like* quick *and* rough *into adverbs* (quickly, roughly) *which explain how or when an action is performed.*

Development

Write words on the board and discuss with the children how we can add the suffix -*y*. Encourage the children to write the root word and then re-write the word adding the suffix. It may be helpful if children write these words in a table (see Table 10.1).

Table 10.1 Adding -*y*

Root word	Suffix
fun	
run	
sun	
yum	
fog	
rain	
mist	
storm	
wind	

As children complete the table, ask them to dot and dash the sounds they can hear. It is essential that throughout spelling lessons children continue to revise phonic sounds and can continue to use these confidently. Depending on their ability, you may give children the root word only to add the suffix or leave the suffix only and the children have to identify the root word.

Once children feel confident about words ending with -y, ask them to identify correct spellings in sentences, by choosing from alternatives. These could be sentences written on the board that children write out or you could provide a worksheet and ask them to circle the correct answer. Your choice will be determined by the children's needs (lower attaining children will not benefit from copying sentences and this could turn into a long task rather than a simple assessment tool). Examples might include:

A dalmatian is a spotty/spoty dog.

It is warm outside because it is suny/sunny.

When it is windy the sea is choppy/chopy.

Commentary

At this stage, children should see that as you add the suffix -y, the single consonant grapheme before the y doubles. To extend higher attaining children, you may wish to dictate the sentences and encourage children to write them rather than simply choosing the correct spelling. Remember, however, that there is a different 'rule' for words that have a split vowel digraph, such as laze *and* craze. *This may be something children could explore in a spelling investigation (see above).*

Putting the word into context

Encourage children, in pairs, to say some of the words they have been learning and to put them into sentences orally before writing them down. You may also want children to place the root words into sentences. This will give you a chance to check that they understand that for some words -y is a suffix. Encourage children to discuss their sentences so that they understand there are many ways to use a word in the correct context.

Testing spelling

Some schools prefer to send home a list of words each week for children to learn. Traditionally, this is marked by the teacher and a score is given. Some teachers decide not to give a list, but to get partners to test each other based on the words learnt that week. They would also mark these together, discussing any mistakes they have made. This could also be done informally with words written on the board (spelled correctly and incorrectly). Children write down the words that are spelled correctly and note down any words that they have found difficult to revise with a partner.

If lists of words are to be given for children to learn, you and the children may find it helpful to hold a 'test' at the beginning of the week before the children see the lists. They can then identify the parts of words they need to learn, and you can see if they already know the words in their lists and, if they do, provide them with different words.

> ## Commentary
>
> *It is important to remember that testing spelling is not the same as teaching spelling. Tests should be used to check on children's learning and to assess what they need to enable them to make progress. In the past, some teachers thought that they had taught spelling because they had given children lists of words to learn and had then tested them. It is essential that children learn how to learn spellings and have strategies for working out how to spell unfamiliar words. Testing alone will not provide such strategies.*

Strategies for learning spellings

It is especially important to provide children and parents/carers with strategies for learning spellings. The might include the following.

- Look, say, cover, write, check: children look at a word, say it out loud, cover it up, attempt to write it correctly, check to see if they are correct. If not, they can repeat the process.

- Identifying the tricky part of a word: if, as suggested above, children have a mock 'test' before attempting to learn the words, they will be able to focus on the tricky parts when learning them.

Next lesson

Adding the suffix -*ly*

Revise previous words/rules

On cards, write the words children have been learning, and then show these cards with children reading the words. Discuss the patterns they can see. Revise the last spelling pattern: adding the suffix -*y*. Can children recall these words and use them in a sentence? Ask children to check their books and revise (using look, say, cover, write, check) any words that they found difficult to spell.

Introducing the pattern/rule

Introduce that this week they will be adding the suffix -*ly* to root words. Often, though not always, adding -*ly* turns words into adverbs (e.g. the adjectives *quick, slow, rapid* change to adverbs when -*ly* is added). Children will need to know what an adverb is.

Commentary

Adverbs are used to modify a verb, an adjective, or another adverb:

A. *Jo runs quickly.*
B. *Sam is an extremely clever boy.*
C. *The car goes incredibly fast.*

In A the adverb quickly *tells us how Jo runs. In B,* extremely *tells us the degree to which Sam is clever. In C, the adverb* incredibly *tells us how fast the car goes.*

Adverbs tell us how, in what way, when, where, and to what extent.

Introduce the word *glad*: *glad* + *ly* makes the adverb *gladly*.

You will also need to explain to children that when adding -*ly* to a word that ends in *y* they need to swap the *y* for an *i*, for example, *easy – easily, happy – happily*.

Identifying sounds within the word

Ask children to identify sounds within the words below and complete Table 10.2. They should discuss the meaning of these words. Can they think of any words to which the suffix -*ly* can be added?

Table 10.2   Adding -*ly*

Root	Suffix
brave	
	normally
quick	
sad	
happy	

Did they remember to swap the *y* for an *i* in *happily*?

Follow this by asking them to identify the correct spelling for examples such as:

He bravely/bravly stepped towards the dragon.

Quietly/quietely she tiptoed towards the door.

He quickely/quickly sprinted towards the finish line.

Once children have identified the correct spelling using cards (you will need to make these in advance) with the root word plus suffix, for example, *glad – gladly*, ask them to say a word to their partner who should say and then write a sentence using that word.

Get children to put words into context by asking them to identify which word they need to use within the sentence: the root word or the adverb. For example:

He played the guitar badly/bad.

She closed the door quietly/quiet.

The prince and princess lived happy/happily ever after.

He was a slowly/slow driver.

The rain fell heavy/heavily.

Peer assessment

Ask children to say the root word and their partner to write the root word plus suffix. As they complete this, children mark each other's work. Ask them to note down any words they may have found difficult to revise in the next lesson. Children should take this opportunity to also test each other on words they may have spelled incorrectly in previous spelling tests.

Teaching Key Stage 2 children who may need support

Children will need to revise the 44 speech sounds and should revisit these if they do not know them. They should be able to use these sounds confidently and apply them within words. If the school follows a programme, you should adapt the words and simplify those where possible. This means that children are still meeting their National Curriculum targets but they are able to use simplified sounds.

Children will also need to catch up. This should be done through support within class, daily support while reading, and identifying gaps in knowledge. When reading to them and with them, discuss spelling patterns, for example *fun* and *funny*, identifying that the *y* represents the 'ee' sound. Once you have discussed the words, show them other words with the same pattern. Write these on cards or in a book and revise these daily where possible.

Learning outcomes review

You should now have a clear understanding of how to build upon children's phonic knowledge to support their spelling, and be able to identify how we use phonics to support spelling. You should also be aware of strategies to teach spelling patterns.

Answers to making -y words plural activity (page 117)
If a vowel precedes the *y* add an *s* (*boys, keys, days, monkeys, donkeys*); if a consonant precedes the *y*, drop the *y* and add *-ies* (*babies, ladies, daisies, bodies*). This rule has hardly any exceptions and the only one we know is *money* and *monies*, a word virtually no-one ever uses anyway.

Further reading

Allott, K (2014) Spelling, in Waugh, D, Jolliffe, W and Allott, K (eds.) *Primary English for Trainee Teachers.* London: SAGE.

Provides guidance on teaching spelling.

Crystal, D (2012) *Spell It Out: The Singular Story of English Spelling.* London: Profile Books.

Provides a fascinating insight into the reasons for English spelling patterns.

Jolliffe, W and Waugh, D with Carss, A (2015) *Teaching Systematic Synthetic Phonics in Primary Schools* (2nd edn.). London: SAGE.

See especially Chapter 6.

Waugh, D, Warner, C and Waugh, R (2013) *Teaching Grammar, Punctuation and Spelling in Primary Schools.* London: SAGE.

See especially Chapters 3, 4 and 5.

Waugh, D, Allott, K, Waugh, R, English, E and Bulmer, E (2014) *The Spelling, Punctuation and Grammar App*. Morecambe: Children Count Ltd. (available through the App Store).

References

Department for Children, Schools and Families (DCSF) (2009) *Support for Spelling.* Norwich: DCSF.

Department for Education (DfE) (2013) *The National Curriculum in England: Framework Document.* London: DfE.

Department for Education and Skills (DfES) (2007) *Letters and Sounds: Principles and Practice of High Quality Phonics.* London: DfES.

Nelson English Skills. Available at: **https://global.oup.com/education/content/primary/series/ nelson-family/?region=international**

Read Write Inc. Spelling. Available at: **www.ruthmiskin.com/en/read-write-inc-programmes/ spelling**

Chapter 11

Teaching tricky or common exception words

Learning outcomes

The chapter will provide ideas for the teaching of the reading and spelling of *tricky* or *common exception* words and how this can be integrated into phonics lessons, and also embedded and applied in teaching across the curriculum.

This chapter will allow you to achieve the following outcomes:

- understand what is meant by tricky or common exception words;
- be aware of strategies for teaching and learning these words;
- understand the importance of emphasising grapheme–phoneme correspondences, even where these are unusual or have yet to be taught and learned.

Teachers' Standards

Working through this chapter will help you meet the following standards:

3. Demonstrate good subject and curriculum knowledge:

- Have a secure knowledge of the relevant subject(s) and curriculum areas, foster and maintain pupils' interest in the subject, and address misunderstandings.
- Demonstrate a critical understanding of developments in the subject and curriculum areas, and promote the value of scholarship.
- Demonstrate an understanding of and take responsibility for promoting high standards of literacy, articulacy and the correct use of standard English, whatever the teacher's specialist subject.
- If teaching early reading, demonstrate a clear understanding of systematic synthetic phonics.

Words, words, words

In this chapter you will find strategies for teaching and learning words that present problems due to their phonic irregularities, or because they include grapheme–phoneme correspondences which children have not met by the time they need to read and write some common words.

Rather than using the term 'tricky words', which occurs throughout government-backed resources such as Letters and Sounds (DfES, 2007), as well as in phonics programmes such as Read Write Inc. (Miskin, 2011), the 2013 National Curriculum uses the term 'common exception words'. The curriculum requires children in Year 1 *to read common exception words, noting unusual correspondences between spelling and sound and where these occur in the word* (DfE, 2013, p20). It is important to remember that, whatever we call them, *words* are not tricky, only parts of some of them are.

For example, look at the word *said*. We can separate the word into its three phonemes and represent them with graphemes: /s/ai/d/. The beginning and ending of the word are highly regular, but the medial vowel sound is represented by 'ai', which is virtually unique in English spelling, and which usually makes an 'ay' sound as in *rain, gain* and *pain*.

So when children learn how to spell *said*, they need to know that it includes a 'tricky part' and learn that it is represented by 'ai' rather than, say, the much more common 'e' or 'ea' (*red, bed, head, read*). Johnston and Watson (2007) maintain that children's attention should be drawn to the *pronounceable elements* of 'tricky' words and point out that *even the word yacht ... has a first and last letter which gives a guide to pronunciation* (pp36–7).

To help you to understand some of the strategies needed to be able to read and spell tricky words, try the activity below.

Activity: Identifying the tricky parts of words

Look at the words below, segment them into their individual phonemes, and identify the parts you need to learn in order to spell them – the tricky bits!

diarrhoea   yacht   design   separate

In English, almost every phoneme can be represented in more than one way. Look at the following examples:

/or/ – cork, pour, haul, paw, ball, taught, thought, score

/s/ – sip, cell, pass, scene, psychology, dance

/sh/ – shop, chef, conscience, spacious, initiative, sugar

This is often used as an argument for not placing a strong emphasis on teaching phonics, but without understanding that sounds are represented by letters, how would we ever be able to spell? Besides, English actually has regular spellings for 80–90% of its words (Adams, 1990; Crystal, 2005), so we can teach children phoneme–grapheme correspondences, which will enable them to decode successfully.

Research focus: Why is English spelling sometimes difficult?

Masha Bell (2011) explains the irregularities of English spelling as follows.

> *It is well known that English words derive mainly from old German and Norman French, and that its alphabet of 26 letters makes it impossible to represent its 43½ speech sounds with just one symbol. But that is not why many English spellings, such as 'daughter', 'brought' and 'people', are now irregular, while their German and French relatives have much better spellings (Tochter, brachte, peuple).*

> *The pronunciations of all three languages have changed since 1066. But only in English have numerous spellings become highly unreliable guides to pronunciation (sound, southern, soup), and spellings for identical sounds have ended up exceptionally varied (blue, shoe, flew, through, to, you, two, too, gnu).*

> *The consistency of English spelling was first seriously corrupted during the reinstatement of English as the official language of England in the 15th century. It suffered even more at the hands of foreign printers during the bible wars of the 16th century. Sadly, there has never been a serious, co-ordinated attempt to remedy the various accidental and deliberate corruptions of the alphabetic principle (of representing speech sounds in a regular manner) in English.*

So our often seemingly illogical spelling system is the result of a series of historical events, which also include invasions such as those by the Romans, Saxons, Vikings and Normans, all of whom brought their languages with them. Our language is a mixture of many different languages, which have many different ways of sounding phonemes. While this means that our language is rich, with many different words for things, it also means that spelling can be challenging, especially for people learning the language.

Activity: The /k/ phoneme

Look at the words below and identify the /k/ sound in each one.

king   back   school

How many other ways can the /k/ phoneme be represented?

Note that some of the less common /k/ graphemes appear in words which have recently come into use from other languages.

The vagaries of the English alphabetic system led to the formation, more than 100 years ago, of the Simplified Spelling Society, which campaigns for greater regularity in spelling. Indeed, in 1906, US President Teddy Roosevelt tried to get the US government to simplify the spelling of 300 common English words. Neither Congress nor the public were enthusiastic about the changes and they didn't happen, although some US spellings have been simplified over the years (*color, harbor, program,* etc). Similar changes did not occur in Britain, so we are left with some challenges when teaching even the most common words in our language.

What are the commonest words?

Even many of our most common words, the ones we cannot say or write a sentence without, include tricky parts. Masterson *et al.* (2003) identified the 100 most common words in the English language (Table 11.1).

Table 11.1 The 100 most common words in the English language, in order of frequency

the	are	do	about	and
up	me	got	a	had
down	their	to	my	dad
people	said	her	big	your
in	what	when	put	he
there	it's	could	I	out
see	house	of	this	looked
old	it	have	very	too
was	went	look	by	you
be	don't	day	they	like
come	made	on	some	will
time	she	so	into	I'm
is	not	back	if	for
then	from	help	at	were
children	Mrs	his	go	him
called	but	little	Mr	here
that	as	get	off	with
no	just	asked	all	mum
now	saw	we	one	came
make	can	them	oh	an

Activity: Common tricky words

Look at the list of the 100 commonest English words in Table 11.1 and identify those which include 'tricky' bits for early readers. Remember that some words may be tricky for children at early stages in their phonic development, but will become easier to decode as they acquire more phonic knowledge.

Research focus: Common exception words and the muddle over tricky words

Mike Lloyd-Jones, the co-author of the Sounds Together Synthetic Phonics Programme, discusses tricky words and teachers' misconceptions about how to teach them as follows.

> Some words use the alphabetic code in a very idiosyncratic way – the way in which the letters represent one or more of the sounds in those words is either more-or-less unique to that word or else is used in only a very small number of words. If these words were all rare or unusual words they could be dealt with later on as schooling progresses, but some of these words are very common and children will meet them frequently in their reading. So children need to be able to read these words and they are taught as 'common exception words'.

> These common exception words all use the alphabet to represent the sounds in those words, but the coding is uncommon or exceptional. So children need to be shown how the alphabetic code works in those words so that they can learn to decode them when they meet them in their reading. These words should not be taught as words to be learned as 'wholes', to be recognised as a single visual pattern or as words for which 'phonics doesn't work'. When children are being shown how the alphabetic code works in these common exception words they are being taught this new bit of code specifically to be able to read those particular words.

> But as well as words with very rare grapheme–phoneme correspondences the category of tricky words also includes many words that use the sound spelling system in a way that is very common but is usually taught as part of the complex code in Year 1. Yet some of these 'tricky words' are very common and children will encounter them frequently even in quite simple texts. So those tricky high-frequency words have to be taught in Reception, in advance of the more general teaching of the relevant grapheme–phoneme correspondences in Year 1.

> The same principle applies to the teaching of these words. Children should be taught how the sound-spelling system works in these words so that they can decode them when they meet them in their reading. These words are not to be taught as 'sight words', they are words that can be 'sounded out' just like any other words once children have been taught the additional phonic knowledge needed for these words. At this stage the phonic knowledge is being taught for word-specific application, but later on (probably in Year 1) they will encounter the same piece of phonic knowledge and see how it is used more widely in other words.

(Lloyd-Jones, 2014)

In the next section, you can see how children's attention can be drawn to the parts of words that they may find tricky at some stages of their phonic development.

Grapheme–phoneme correspondences: 'Grotty graphemes'

The phonics programme Read Write Inc. uses the term 'grotty grapheme' for the graphemes that make a word 'tricky'. In the list below, Waugh and Harrison-Palmer (2013) have identified the 'grotty graphemes' in some of the most common words.

> w<u>a</u>s: 'a' grapheme represents an 'o' sound rather than the short vowel sound it usually represents.
>
> ha<u>ve</u>: this is not a split digraph. Instead the 've' grapheme makes the 'v' sound.
>
> n<u>o</u>: 'o' grapheme represents the long vowel sound rather than the short vowel.
>
> h<u>e</u>: 'e' grapheme represents the long vowel sound rather than the short vowel sound.
>
> y<u>ou</u>: 'ou' grapheme represents an 'oo' sound which is a less common grapheme–phoneme correspondence and has not been taught in phase two or three.
>
> d<u>ay</u>: 'ay' grapheme represents an 'ai' sound. This grapheme–phoneme correspondence has not been taught in phase two or three.
>
> w<u>ere</u>: 'ere' grapheme represents an 'ur' sound. This grapheme–phoneme correspondence has not been taught in phase two or three.
>
> y<u>our</u>: 'our' grapheme represents an 'or' sound. This grapheme–phoneme correspondence has not been taught in phase two or three.
>
> h<u>ere</u>: 'ere' grapheme represents an 'ear' sound. This grapheme–phoneme correspondence has not been taught in phase two or three.
>
> th<u>ey</u>: 'ey' grapheme represents an 'ai' sound which is a less common grapheme–phoneme correspondence and has not been taught in phase two or three.

(Waugh and Harrison-Palmer, 2013, pp16–17)

Heather, a literacy co-ordinator who teaches phonics through Read Write Inc. commented:

> Children are taught from YR to identify 'grotty graphemes' and to discuss why they are 'grotty'. These words are red in RWI books so children don't try to apply phonic decoding strategies. In every lesson, children are reminded about the red words and they are discussed frequently, displayed and referred to daily. I think it is the constant, early exposure and discussion to ensure understanding that is key for success with this scheme.

The *Jolly Phonics Readers* (2012) introduce the tricky words in groups, each level building on the words learned in the previous level. Children should be taught the tricky words for each level before they are asked to read the books at that level (see Table 11.2).

Table 11.2 Jolly Phonics – in stages

Red Level	Yellow Level	Green Level		Blue Level	
I	are	go	live	any	could
the	all	no	give	many	should
he	you	so	little	more	would
she	your	my	down	before	right
me	come	one	what	other	two
we	some	by	when	were	four
be	said	only	why	because	goes
was	here	old	where	want	does
to	there	like	who	saw	made
do	they	have	which	put	their
of					

Source: http://jollylearning.co.uk/gallery/handy-tricky-word-list

Notice how many words are grouped together because they have common features, for example *he, she, me, we* and *be; come, some; go, no, so; what, when, why, where, who, which; could, would, should.*

Homophones and heteronyms

Homophones

The English language has many words that sound the same but are spelled differently (*homophones* – meaning 'same sound', from the Greek *homos*, 'same', and *phone*, meaning 'sound'). Look at the words below:

wee, bee, ah, ewe, hear, know, sew, watt, wear, witch, sore, write, putt

We only know how to spell some of the words if we have some context for them. If you heard these words without seeing them and were asked to spell them, you might write:

we, be, are, you, here, no, so, what, where, which, saw, right, put

We need context for words if we are to be sure to spell them correctly.

English vocabulary is rich with homophones, which give us many of our jokes such as:

What's black and white and red (read) all over? – A newspaper!

So *read* is the past tense of the verb 'to read' (*I read the book last week*) and red is a colour (*a red shirt*). For children learning to read and spell, homophones can present problems and cause misunderstandings. Support for Spelling maintains that in Year 4 children should learn *to distinguish between the spelling and meaning of homophones* (DCSF, 2009, p4), and advocates learning homophones alongside other words with similar spellings rather than alongside other homophones.

So we might teach *where* alongside *here* and *there* rather than alongside *wear*. Other examples could include:

- teaching *there* with *here* and *where* – because all are words to do with location and have a similar spelling pattern;

- teaching *their* with *heir* and an explanation that this is an unusual way of spelling the /air/ phoneme;

- teaching *they're* with other contractions, such as *I'm, you're, he's, she's, we're*;

- teaching *lead* (the metal) with *bread, instead, head*;

- teaching *led* (the verb, past tense) with *fed, shed, bed*.

Even if we explain the different word meanings when teaching homophones together (e.g. *there, their* and *they're*), children get the message that these are words which are easily confused, and as a result they do confuse them. Mudd (1994) maintained that grouping homophones together worked well for good spellers (who were likely already to know the different spellings), but not for weaker spellers.

Heteronyms

Just to confuse matters further, English vocabulary includes several heteronyms: words that are spelled the same but pronounced differently and have different meanings.

Consider how you would pronounce *record* and how different pronunciations would give different meanings to the word.

Consider the following words and how you would say them and what they mean. What would you need to know to ensure that you pronounced them correctly and understood their meanings?

read   sow   lead   close   rebel   desert   minute   present

As children learn more about homophones and heteronyms and become confident about their spellings, they might go on to make collections and even create their own jokes involving a play on words or misunderstandings, but for early readers and spellers this might prove confusing.

Content words

Many of the most commonly used words are short ones whose main purpose is to join other words in sentences, so they are called 'function words' (see Table 11.1). If we are unable to read and write them, our language experiences will be restricted. Other words give us meaning in sentences by naming and describing things and actions: these are known as 'content words'.

When children first begin to recognise words around them it is usually the content words that they can first read. After all, there is an incentive to be able to read words like ice cream, pizza and toys! It is important that the commonest functional words are learned alongside content words so that as children's phonological understanding grows they are able to read sentences and longer pieces of text. The most commonly used nouns, verbs and adjectives are shown in Table 11.3.

Table 11.3   The most common nouns, verbs and adjectives

Nouns	Verbs	Adjectives
1 time	1 be	1 good
2 person	2 have	2 new
3 year	3 do	3 first
4 way	4 say	4 last
5 day	5 get	5 long
6 thing	6 make	6 great
7 man	7 go	7 little
8 world	8 know	8 own
9 life	9 take	9 other
10 hand	10 see	10 old
11 part	11 come	11 right
12 child	12 think	12 big
13 eye	13 look	13 high
14 woman	14 want	14 different
15 place	15 give	15 small
16 work	16 use	16 large
17 week	17 find	17 next
18 case	18 tell	18 early
19 point	19 ask	19 young
20 government	20 work	20 important
21 company	21 seem	21 few
22 number	22 feel	22 public
23 group	23 try	23 bad
24 problem	24 leave	24 same
25 fact	25 call	25 able

Source: **www.oxforddictionaries.com/words/the-oec-facts-about-the-language**

Activity: Content words

Look at the content words in Table 11.3 and identify those that contain tricky bits which may need to be learned. Do this by reading each word and then segmenting it into its phonemes and matching these to the graphemes that represent them. Ask yourself the following questions.

- Which words are regular and could be spelled by a child who has reached Phase 6 of Letters and Sounds?
- Which words have one irregular sound–symbol correspondence?
- Which have more than one irregular sound–symbol correspondence?

Strategies for learning tricky or common exception words

There are two key things we need to do to support children's learning of common words:

1. Draw attention to the words and their spellings through frequent exposure.

2. Draw attention to the tricky parts of the words to help them to learn to read and spell them.

The activities described below are designed to support such learning.

Matching games

Children need to become very familiar with common exception words, so games that require them to find pairs of words, such as snap or concentration, are invaluable. Simply make cards with common words on them and ask children to make pairs using a range of game formats.

Before they start, get them to look at all the word cards and, if necessary with help, say them out loud. Encourage them to say the words when they make a pair and follow activities by asking them to write on the wall the words in their winning 'tricks'. For content words they could write the word and draw a picture to represent it.

Rhymes

Earlier in the chapter you saw how important it is not to confuse children by teaching homophones together. When working on rhymes for common words, emphasise those rhymes that have similar spellings for the rime of the words. (The rime is the part of a word that makes the rhyme, so -ack in black, track and crack; -ing in wing, sing and ring.) You will find that some of the common content words have very few rhymes that are spelled in the same way (for example, eye, work and world), but most have several possible rhymes that children may know (try, for example, way, part and place).

Dictation and cloze work

Produce short pieces of text with missing words that children can insert, either by reading the text and then choosing from a selection of common words or by listening to the text being read aloud as they follow it and then choosing from a selection of words. This type of activity is best done in pairs or small groups to encourage discussion and debate and to share knowledge and understanding.

Texts should not have too many words removed or they will be difficult for children to 'get into'. Ideally, you should take out no more than one in ten words.

Using the school environment

One school has painted common exception words on bricks in the playground. Children play games in lessons such as having word cards with Blu-tack or a similar reusable adhesive putty on the back and having to place as many as possible next to a matching word on a brick in a given time. The school found that some children developed their own games at playtimes and that this was reinforcing children's ability to read and spell the words. Indeed, children asked if they could make their own cards and if the teachers would paint more words on bricks so that they could develop their games.

Mnemonics (pronounced nemonics)

If you have read Roald Dahl's *Matilda*, you will know that Matilda's teacher, Miss Honey, helped children to learn how to spell tricky words by teaching them mnemonics such as:

Mrs D

Mrs I

Mrs FFI

Mrs C

Mrs U

Mrs LTY

(Dahl, 1988, p141)

Many teachers help children to learn spellings using mnemonics such as 'Big Elephants Can Always Use Some Energy' for *because*, and 'I shall be your friend to the end' to remember that *friend* ends with *end* and that the *i* comes before the *e*. Mnemonics can be individual ways of remembering words which cause the writer particular problems, such as 'a PIEce of pie' for *piece*, or 'oh you lucky duck' for *would, could* and *should*.

Adults, too, use mnemonics for spelling, including 'stationery has envelopes' to recall that there is an *e* before the *r*, while *stationary*, meaning 'still', has an *a*; and 'Run Run Hurry Or Else Accident' to remember the tricky part of the spelling of *diarrhoea*!

Mnemonics can be useful if used sparingly, but children may sometimes find it harder to remember the mnemonic than the spelling!

Try asking your class to devise their own mnemonics to help them to spell tricky words. Make a collection and share them with colleagues. One school came up with:

does   dogs only eat sausages

goes   gorillas often eat sausages

was   wasps always sting

any   ants never yawn

many   many ants never yawn

they   they eat yoghurt

said   Sally Ann is dreaming

Teachers then asked children to create mnemonics for other words to add to the list and create a spelling display in the school hall.

Actions to accompany words

Look at the verbs and adjectives in the content words list. Choose those which your class might find challenging and play games where you show a word and they produce actions to represent it. From the verbs, try *give, work, try* and *call* and think about the actions you could make. Next, try some adjectives such as *great, old, young* and *high*. Teachers who use this approach report that children ask to use it when they learn new words and that the activity is sometimes incorporated into drama lessons.

Visualisation strategies

When our eyes move they access different parts of the brain in relation to the past, future, sight, sound and feelings (see Grinder *et al.*, 1980). Typically, eyes move upwards to access the part of the brain that processes visual images, down for feelings, and remain level for sound. If you can calibrate how different individuals' eyes connect to different parts of the brain, then you can communicate more effectively with them. In relation to spelling, it is possible to train someone to spell by the language you use and by encouraging them to look up to access the part of the brain that processes visual images.

Neuro-linguistic Programming (NLP) makes use of visual imagery, so when teaching a tricky word:

- write the word on card, large and clear;

- hold the card in front of the child (above their eye line);

- discuss the visual appearance of the word with the child and any particular features;

- then ask the child to visualize the word;

- remove the card and encourage the child to name the letters forwards and backwards;

- if any mistakes are made, look again at the card and point out notable features;

- then ask the child to write the word, naming the letters, then look at the card again.

A visual strategy for spelling works well because it is less prone to guesswork. If you visualise the word *fewer* using the process above, you will actually see the letters in the word. If you hear the word and try to apply phonic strategies, there are several possibilities. If you look down, as weaker spellers often do, you are feeling the word and therefore the spelling attempt will be based on 'gut feeling' or guess work and so the attempt will, more often than not, be unsuccessful. If we can teach children to visualise the common exception words, then we are providing them with an additional strategy for spelling, especially when the words are not encodable phonetically.

Another idea which links with this is illustrating the word in some way, for example writing the word 'rain' with raindrops around it in order to help children to create that visual image in the first instance.

Spelling tests

Many schools, where children are given lists of words to learn for tests, give children the 'test' before they see the list they have to learn. This enables children to have a go at the spellings and to identify those they already know and what the tricky bits are in those they can't yet spell accurately. They can then focus their learning on what they actually need to remember, such as *separate* has 'a rat' in it, and *thumb* ends with a *b*.

Conclusion

Most tricky or common exception words can be learnt using a combination of phonic strategies. It is important to emphasise that all words have grapheme–phoneme correspondences for every phoneme, even though some of these may be unusual.

For example, in the word *people* the /ee/ sound is represented by the digraph /eo/, a combination of letters which actually occurs in almost 2,000 English words (*geography, stereo, pigeon, yeoman*, etc.), but hardly ever to represent an /ee/ sound (*diarrhoea* is a rare example). Nevertheless, when explaining how to spell and read the word *people*, you should point out that /ee/ is represented by 'eo', while explaining that this is very unusual.

Allowing children time to explore, discover and discuss common exception words is pivotal to their development as spellers. Providing a range of strategies to help children remember, and ensuring frequent exposure to these words, will assist in breaking down the barriers to spelling.

Learning outcomes review

You should now understand what is meant by tricky or common exception words and be aware of strategies for teaching and learning these words. You should also understand the importance of emphasising grapheme-phoneme correspondences, even where these are unusual or have yet to be taught and learned.

Answers to the identifying tricky parts activity (page 127)

You were asked to look at the words below, segment them into their individual phonemes, and identify the parts you need to learn in order to spell them – the tricky bits!

- *diarrhoea* – virtually all of this word is tricky apart from *di* and *a*. The word is often learned through mnemonics such as 'Run Run Hurry Or Else Accident'!

- *yacht* – *y* and *t* are regular with 'ach' representing the 'o' sound.

- *design* – the final two phonemes are tricky. A good way to learn words with a silent *g* is to look at and sound out words derived from them where the *g* is sounded, for example: *design – designate, resign – resignation*.

- *separate* – the tricky bit is the *a* between *p* and *r*, which people often spell with an 'e'. The mnemonic separate has 'a rat' in it that can help – *sep* a rat *e*.

Answers to the *k* phoneme activity (page 128)
You were asked to look at the words below and identify the /k/ sound in each.

- <u>k</u>ing
- ba<u>ck</u>
- s<u>ch</u>ool

How many other ways can the /k/ phoneme be represented? Examples could include:

- Ira<u>q</u>
- a<u>cc</u>ount
- <u>c</u>at
- tre<u>kk</u>er
- che<u>qu</u>e
- bou<u>qu</u>et

Answers to common tricky words activity (page 129)
Letters and Sounds (DfES, 2007) identified the following common words, which cannot be sounded out phonetically at an early stage and are therefore harder to teach and learn. Many have irregular and uncommon phoneme–grapheme correspondences.

the	me	said	little	Mrs
to	be	have	one	looked
I	was	like	when	called
no	you	so	out	asked
go	they	do	what	could
into	all	some	oh	
he	are	come	their	
she	my	were	people	
we	her	there	Mr	

Answers to content words activity (page 134)
You were asked to look at the content words listed and identify those that contain tricky bits which may need to be learned. Do this by reading each word and then

segmenting it into its phonemes and matching these to the graphemes that represent them. You were asked:

- Which words are regular and could be spelled by a child who had reached Phase 6 of Letters and Sounds?

  time, year, way, day, thing, man, life, hand, part, place, week, case, point, number, problem, fact, be, do, say, get, make, go, take, see, think, look, use, tell, ask, seem, feel, try, leave, call, good, new, first, last, long, little, own, old, right, big, high, different, small, large, next, important, few, public, bad, same, able

- Which words have one irregular sound–symbol correspondence?

  world, child, eye, government, company, group, have, know, come, want, give, find, work, great, other, early, young

- Which have more than one irregular sound–symbol correspondence?

  woman

Further reading

For helpful ideas try Cippenham Infant School's website: **www.cippenhaminfantschool.co.uk/ wp-content/uploads/2009/04/Strategies-for-Tricky-Words.pdf**

References

Adams, MJ (1990) *Beginning to Read: Learning and Thinking about Print.* London: MIT.

Bell, M (2011) Available at: **http://spellingsociety.org/irregularities-of-english-spelling#/page/1** [accessed 19 May 2015].

Crystal, D (2005) *How Language Works.* London: Penguin.

Dahl, R (1988) *Matilda.* London: Jonathan Cape.

Department for Education (DfE) (2013) *The National Curriculum in England: Framework Document.* London: DfE.

Department for Education and Skills (DfES) (2007) *Letters and Sounds: Principles and Practice of High Quality Phonics.* London: DfES.

Grinder, J, Bandler, R, DeLozier, J and Dilts, R (1980) *Neuro-linguistic Programming: The Study of the Structure of Subjective Experience, Volume I.* Capitola, CA: Meta Publications.

Johnston, R and Watson, J (2007) *Teaching Synthetic Phonics.* Exeter: Learning Matters.

Jolly Phonics Readers (2012) Jolly Learning Ltd. Available at: **www.jollylearning.co.uk** [accessed 19 May 2015].

Lloyd-Jones, C and Lloyd-Jones, M. Sounds Together Synthetic Phonics Programme. Available at: **www.soundstogether.co.uk** [accessed 18 May 2015].

Lloyd-Jones, M (2014) *Common Exception Words and the Muddle over Tricky Words.* The Phonics Blog. Available at: **www.phonicsblog.co.uk/#/blog/4565770755/Common-Exception-Words-and-the-Muddle-over-Tricky-Words/7631625** [accessed 19 May 2015].

Masterson, J, Stuart, M, Dixon, M and Lovejoy, S (2003) *Children's Printed Word Database.* Economic and Social Research Council funded project (Ref. R00023406). Nottingham: DCSF.

Miskin, R (2011) *Read Write Inc.: Phonics Handbook.* Oxford: Oxford University Press.

Mudd, N (1994) *Effective Spelling.* London: Hodder and Stoughton/UKRA.

Oxford Dictionaries website. Available at: **www.oxforddictionaries.com/words/the-oec-facts-about-the-language** [accessed 6 April 2015].

Waugh, D and Harrison-Palmer, R (2013) *Teaching Systematic Synthetic Phonics: Audit and Test.* London: SAGE.

Chapter 12

Moving on

Learning outcomes

This chapter will allow you to achieve the following outcomes:

- explore ways in which phonics can be taught;
- identify useful resources that can be used to support teaching and learning;
- be aware of the school environment's potential for developing children's phonemic awareness.

Teachers' Standards

Working through this chapter will help you meet the following standards:

2. Promote good progress and outcomes by pupils:

- Be accountable for pupils' attainment, progress and outcomes.
- Be aware of pupils' capabilities and their prior knowledge, and plan teaching to build on these.

3. Demonstrate good subject and curriculum knowledge:

- Demonstrate an understanding of and take responsibility for promoting high standards of literacy, articulacy and the correct use of standard English, whatever the teacher's specialist subject.
- Have a secure knowledge of the relevant subject(s) and curriculum areas, foster and maintain pupils' interest in the subject, and address misunderstandings.

Introduction

In this chapter you will find suggestions for developing your repertoire of ideas and activities for teaching phonics. You should be constantly on the lookout for new and stimulating teaching strategies and be willing to share your own ideas with colleagues. The Rose Review maintained that:

Phonic work should be set within a broad and rich language curriculum that takes full account of developing the four interdependent strands of language: speaking, listening, reading and writing and enlarging children's stock of words.

(Rose, 2006, p70)

Creating the right environment

Throughout this book we have tried to place phonics teaching and learning within the wider context of a broad, rich language environment, with lessons designed not only to help children learn the basic phonics skills but also to engage them with texts and encourage them to enjoy reading and talking about texts.

To achieve this in your classroom and beyond you will need to create a literate environment in which children have ready access to a wide range of texts and in which language, both oral and written, is a source of pleasure. Below you will find some examples of things successful teachers have done to create broad and rich language environments and remember to refer back to the ideas in Chapter 2, 'Phonics in context'.

Working walls

Most classrooms have useful and often interactive displays of words on their walls. These might include collections of nouns that include grapheme–phoneme correspondences (GPCs) currently being taught; alliterative phrases; homophones; common words; common exception words; and collections of rhyming words. These displays can be a focal point for teaching and learning and a resource for children to draw upon when they need help with spelling or ideas for their writing. Working walls are designed to build and grow as teaching of a sequence of learning develops. It is useful to include phonics prompts and resources on your maths working wall and your 'topic' working wall so children see learning to read as integral and integrated.

Postcards from teddy

In one class, a teddy bear appeared on a table at the front of the classroom one day and the teacher (who had secretly put it there) asked the children if anyone knew where the bear had come from. No-one knew, so the children were asked to decide on a name for the bear. They discussed and wrote possibilities on mini white boards and the teacher transcribed these, with accurate spellings, onto the board. A vote was held to choose the class's favourite name and the children chose *Ted*.

The next day the bear had 'disappeared' and a note in an envelope had taken his place. It was from Ted, who told the children he had gone on his holidays and would send them postcards if they wrote to him at the address he gave at the seaside. In preparation for this, the teacher had collected postcards from different places and wrote messages from Ted on them in response to children's messages, some of which were the products of shared writing and some written by individuals.

The teacher had also taken Ted to places he had visited or asked friends to do the same, each time taking a photograph of Ted with various items such as a bucket and spade, a small umbrella and a meal or drink. Ted sent the photographs to the class as e-mail attachments with messages for them to respond to.

Eventually, Ted returned and became a fixture in the classroom, but occasionally went on another 'trip' and corresponded with the children. The resultant discussion and writing aroused children's enthusiasm and enabled the teacher to discuss spelling, reading and writing, as well as reinforcing the phonics work the class were engaged in.

Phonics in a class shop

Many classes have shops in which various items (usually as empty packages or plastic fruit and vegetables, etc.) are bought and sold. The shop can be a great resource for maths work, but also for literacy activities. Children can make shopping lists, advertisements for products, notices and signs and lists of things the shop needs to order. In one class, children combined design technology, art and literacy work to create their own boxes for products such as cereals, washing powder and biscuits. They invented names for the products and looked at real packaging to help them decide on contents, advertising blurbs and even nutritional values (but not for the washing powders!).

Digraph shop

In a basket have a selection of items or pictures of items that have *sh* and *ch* in them, for example: *shoe, polish, chips, chocolate, shell, fish, cheese*. Ask children to come and pick items out and tell the class what they are. Write these words on the board as you go along. When the basket is empty, ask children what they notice about all the items (the answer should be that they contain the 'sh' or 'ch' sounds).

Next, ask children to sort the items into a 'sh' pile and a 'ch' pile. Go through each pile asking children to say the name of the item and address any misconceptions.

Go on to introduce other digraphs, both vowel and consonant, when appropriate.

Numbers

Display a chart of the numbers 1 to 10 presented in figures and words (Table 12.1).

Table 12.1 Numbers 1–10

1	2	3	4	5	6	7	8	9	10
one									

Read the rhymes below and ask children to look at the rhyming words at the ends of each line. Ask them to write down pairs of rhyming words from the poems.

> *One, two,*
> *Buckle my shoe.*
> *Three, four,*
> *Knock at the door.*
> *Five, six,*
> *Pick up sticks.*
> *Seven, eight,*
> *Lay them straight.*
> *Nine, ten,*
> *A big fat hen.*
>
> *One, two, three, four, five,*
> *Once I caught a fish alive.*
> *Six, seven, eight, nine, ten,*
> *Then I let it go again.*
> *Why did you let it go?*
> *Because it bit my finger so.*
> *Which finger did it bite?*
> *This little finger on my right.*

Look at the poems and learn them together. Ask children to think of other words that would rhyme with them.

Create a display with the names of the numbers written on an enlarged chart and the class's suggested rhymes written next to them. You could extend this to numbers up to 20 as there are lines for *One, two, buckle my shoe* which go up to 20. Some children might be given these to read and be asked to learn spellings of numbers 11 to 20. Although rhymes for these numbers may be limited, given that so many end with *teen*, this is a good opportunity to reinforce the /ee/ phoneme (see Chapter 5).

Displays

It is important to display children's phonics work. This makes the words you have been learning visible and accessible around the classroom and celebrates children's achievements. In one class, 'phonics snakes' were dangled from the ceiling, attached to windows, stuck onto children's desks or hanging from the wall. The 'snakes' each had a grapheme of a digraph on their heads with a series of words that included that digraph on rings along their bodies. For example, there were snakes with each of the following:

ch: chip, chop, cheese, chase, choose

wh: when, what, why, where

ay: play, stay, way, day, may

Children made their own 'snakes' and enjoyed using simple dictionaries to check that their words existed. For the digraphs that ended words, the teacher linked this work to rhyme and used the snakes as a resource to help children produce simple rhyming verses.

Phonics outdoors

Graphemes on the wall and water pistols

In one school we visited, children enjoyed playing a phonics game involving graphemes painted on an outside wall and water pistols. The teaching assistant gave water pistols to pairs of children in turn and then said a word. Children had to fire water at the grapheme they thought began the word. They developed this into a game they could play by themselves, with children taking turns to say words, including names of television programmes and classmates.

Grapheme hopscotch

Another school adapted hopscotch so that graphemes replaced numbers and they had to 'hop' words. If the example below were used (Table 12.2), this could involve hopping from *s* to *a* to *p* to make *sap*; from *t* to *i* to *n* to make *tin*, etc. For each hop, children say the sound and at the end they say the word they have made.

Table 12.2 Playing hopscotch with graphemes

s	a	n
t	i	p

The graphemes can be changed and a range of 'courts' with different graphemes can be set out in the playground.

Grapheme cards: A basic resource

A set of grapheme cards is a simple but very versatile and effective resource, which can be used at different levels and with different age groups. The example below (Table 12.3) shows a typical set which might be used in Key Stage 1, but which could also be useful in Key Stage 2, especially if further graphemes are added.

Table 12.3   Grapheme cards

s	a	t	i	p	n
s	a	t	i	p	n
c	k	e	h	r	m
c	k	e	h	r	m
g	o	u	l	f	b
g	o	u	l	f	b
a	e	i	o	u	e
e	a	i	d	y	y
d	v	ai	oa	j	ee
ie	or	z	w	ng	oo
y	x	ch	th	igh	oi
ar	ay	ow	ew	u-e	qu
ow	i-e	o-e	sh	aw	ir
ue	oy	ea	a-e	ou	ur

You will see that several graphemes appear more than once. This is because they are common and many of the activities described below require children to create several words. If you only have, for example, one letter *e* (the most common letter in the alphabet), once it has been used children's choices for word building would be severely restricted.

Create a set of grapheme cards by printing them on card and then laminating to preserve them for lots of use, before cutting them into individual cards. Try not to leave much space to the left and right of each grapheme when you cut them out, so that the letters can be placed close to each other to make words.

Grapheme cards activities

Grapheme cards can be used for word building in a variety of ways, ranging from simple starter activities to more challenging games.

Simple starter activities

- For children at the early stages of phonemic awareness, focus on single letters such as *s,a,t,p,i,n* – and do some consonant–vowel–consonant word building.

- Challenge them to see how many words they can make.

- Encourage them to rearrange the letters to make more words.

- Can children substitute a letter for one in a word to make a new word, for example *sit, pit, pat, pan, tan, tin, tip*?

- Move on to or add the next group of single-letter graphemes, for example *c,k,e,h,r,m,d*, and do the same.

- If children can manage this, move on to *g,o,u,l,f,b*.

- Give children the cards to work together to see how many words they can make. Have a dictionary ready to check that the words exist.

- Revise by showing children cards one at a time and asking them to make the sounds and say a word that begins with the sound.

- Go on to ask them to say words that end with the sounds, have the sounds in the middle, etc.

- Include the remaining single-letter graphemes – *z,w,v,y,x*.

Digraphs and trigraphs

- Introduce the digraphs *ng, oo, ch, sh, th* or whichever are addressed first in the phonics programme you use.

- Repeat and develop some of the simple activities above adding these graphemes, or reduce the number of cards and substitute some with the digraphs in word building.

- Introduce *qu, ou, oi, ue, ar*. Build some words using these graphemes.

- Talk about *qu* having two sounds and show how *q* only becomes a 'kw' sound when followed by *u* – see how many words children know beginning with *qu*. Use the opportunity to explain that in English words *q* is always followed by *u*.

- If appropriate, go on to introduce other graphemes – *ay, ea, igh, ow, ew* – and use them for word building.

Split vowel digraphs

- Introduce split vowel digraphs *a-e, i-e, o-e, u-e, e-e*, and see how many words can be made using these. Talk about the effect the final *e* has on the sound of the first vowel and build some words which change pronunciation once an *e* is added to create a split vowel digraph, e.g. *tub – tube, bit – bite, hat – hate, sit – site, them – theme*. When making your split vowel digraph cards, it is a good idea to add a little extra space between the two vowels so that a consonant card can be placed between them without covering either letter up, for example 'a – e' rather than 'a-e'.

Introducing more graphemes

- Introduce *ir, ur, au, aw, al, oy, ow* and *y* as a vowel sound (*my, funny*, etc.).

- Repeat and develop word building activities.

Further activities

- Play bingo by giving children four grapheme cards each. Specify the grapheme–phoneme correspondence you are looking for, for example: *I want a word which begins with a 'sh' sound as in 'shop', I want a word which has an 'ou' sound in the middle as in 'shout'*. Children can turn a card over if they have the appropriate grapheme card and can say a word that fits your description.

- See how many words children can make using two, three and four cards.

- Ask them to try to create even longer words.

- Discuss which graphemes can begin and end words and which usually do not begin words or end words; for example, *ng, igh* and *ie* do not appear at the beginning of words, and *j, v* and *ai* do not appear at the end of English words.

- Encourage children to make up their own games and explain to others how to play them.

Remember that while games should be fun, they need to focus on learning and not distract children from it, so if they spend a lot of time arguing about points scored or turn-taking, they will be less focused on learning. It is important, therefore, that games are supervised when children first play them so that they learn the etiquette expected when playing.

More phonics-based games

Simple matching games might range from snap, using single graphemes and digraphs, to matching words that begin with the same graphemes or those which have similar medial or final sounds. These can be developed for more able readers and for older children. For example, football snap requires children to match football teams that have graphemes and/or phonemes in common. For example, Chelsea and Manchester City could be matched because both have *ch* and *e*. If children make a match, let them make up and read out a football result of their choice, for example: <u>Ch</u>elsea 1 Man<u>ch</u>ester City 2.

Activity: Football matches

Look at the teams below (Table 12.4) and see how many matches you can find. There are lots of possibilities!

(Continued)

(Continued)

Table 12.4 Matching the teams

Aston Villa	Brentford	Brighton	Chelsea
Doncaster Rovers	Everton	Fulham	Ipswich Town
Liverpool	Manchester United	Newcastle United	Stoke City
Sunderland	Swansea City	West Ham United	York City

The above activity can also be done with children's names, names of TV programmes, places and so forth. You could also adapt the game below to use football teams, etc.

Right or wrong snap

This game gives children the opportunity to practise recognising graphemes in both real and pseudo words. Put a set of words on the board (both real and pseudo) and ask children to say them out loud: *stay, toud, cloud, found, play, glay, clay, troud, zay, scout, ploud, tray, vay, proud, froud.*

Ask children to suggest which words could be paired because they have similar sounds or spellings (for example, *toud* and *cloud*). Accept all reasonable suggestions for pairings of words including the same digraphs or the same initial or final sounds.

Give each child a word from the above group or a set which include graphemes they have been learning on a piece of card face up. Have a class game of snap. Write a word on the board and if children think their word pairs with yours they shout 'snap!'

Phonics bingo

This can be played using grapheme cards or whole words. If using grapheme cards, deal each player six cards and then say a series of common words. Each time a player has a grapheme s/he thinks is in the word read out, s/he turns the card over. When all six cards are turned over, the winner shouts 'bingo!' If using whole words, read out graphemes and if a corresponding phoneme appears in a child's word cards s/he can turn it over. Continue until someone gets a full house and calls 'bingo!'

Anagrams of high-frequency words

To focus children's attention on high-frequency words they need to become familiar with, play an anagram game, which draws their attention to the correct spellings.

Choose three children and give each an A4 card with a letter or digraph on it, so that when the cards are arranged in the correct order they make a common word (for example, *all*). Ask others to come and 'rearrange' the children to make the word, thus drawing their attention to what an anagram is (use the term anagram – an additional activity could be to ask the children to suggest how anagram is spelled and display this on the board).

Repeat the activity with other children using different letters to make more common words, for example *tree, house, they, there*.

Short games and activities

When children are lining up to go out to play, etc., play games that involve listening to and repeating sequences of sounds. These could be sequences of claps or animal noises that they can repeat, or even a phonics rap. You can also play an adapted version of I spy; for example, *I hear with my little ear something beginning with 'shhh'* [or *mmm*, etc.]. Not only do these activities reinforce learning and make it enjoyable, but they also hold children's attention at times when class management can be most challenging.

Guess my word

Another activity which can be short and purposeful and done orally or with writing involves the teacher asking children to suggest which word s/he is thinking of. For example, *It ends with a 'lll' sound; it begins with a 'fff' sound. What could it be?* Children might suggest *fill, full, fall, fell*, etc. All plausible answers should be praised, but you can guide them towards the word you are thinking of by giving a clue about its meaning, for example, *You would be this if you had eaten a lot*.

Rhymes

Nursery rhymes, jingles and word games *act as a trigger for raising phonological awareness* (Layton *et al*., 1998, p11). In earlier chapters, you have read about phrases that can be used to embed GPCs: rhymes are even more powerful. Think about some of the rhymes you remember easily and you will see how rhyme helps us to remember things, such as 'Never Eat Shredded Wheat' (NESW are the points of the compass) and for the days in the months:

> *Thirty days hath September,*
>
> *April, June and November.*
>
> *All the rest have thirty-one,*
>
> *except February alone,*
>
> *which has 28 days clear,*
>
> *and 29 each leap year.*

There is an important role for parents and carers in their children's literacy development through sharing rhymes, jingles and songs. This can be done through:

- listening to and saying nursery, number and action rhymes;
- playing games such as *I hear with my little ear something that rhymes with ...*;
- making up stories with rhyming words including nonsense words;
- reading poems to children;
- reading stories which include rhymes to children.

Creating a bank of rhyming words

Explore rhymes with children in preparation for them writing simple poems. Discuss the topic for the poems and ask for suggestions for words they might need, then ask children to think of words to rhyme with as many of the words as possible. They will realise that some words are best not placed at the ends of lines as there are few rhymes for them, while others have lots of possible rhymes and can be placed at the ends of lines.

Exploring rhymes

Even in the simplest and most common rhymes there are often different ways of spelling the same sound. For example, in 'Baa Baa Black Sheep' *wool* rhymes with *full*; in 'Twinkle Twinkle Little Star', *star* rhymes with *are*, and *high* with *sky*; and in 'Little Miss Muffet', *whey* rhymes with *away*. Encourage children to explore rhymes and investigate their spellings. Some will be able to make lists of words that rhyme with the rhymes in jingles and poems according to their spellings. For example, they could create tables like the one below (Table 12.5) for the rhyme: *Which finger did it bite? This little finger on my right.*

Table 12.5 Making rhymes

bite	right
white	night
site	bright
kite	tight
polite	sight
bite	light
	fight
	might
	right

As children explore spellings of rhymes (or 'rimes' as they are sometimes called), they will become increasingly aware of the most likely spellings. For example, there are many more words that have similar spellings to *star* (*bar, car, far, tar, etc.*) than *are*.

Alliteration

Alliteration helps to reinforce phonological and phonemic awareness and can be a source of great amusement to children. Try saying names and asking children to put alliterative adjectives with them (Lucky Lucy, Marvellous Mark, Cheeky Chelsea, etc.). Encourage them to develop these noun phrases into sentences and make a display, which can be a focal point for discussing GPCs.

This will provide an opportunity to discuss some of the variations in sound–symbol correspondences that occur, particularly where names are used. Given that many classes include children with names like Charlotte, Chelsea and Chloe; Sean and Sam; Sophie, Lily and Zoe, children will be increasingly aware that the grapheme–phoneme correspondences they learn in school do not always apply consistently to their names and those of their friends.

Explore deliberate misspellings of brands and bands

Many brand names such as Weetabix, Betabuy, Kwikfit and Kleenex are deliberately misspelled in phonically regular ways. This can be confusing for children learning to spell, but can also be a useful topic for discussion. Collections of packages can be made and included in a class shop and some children might be asked to work out how the names of such products might be spelled if more conventional GPCs were used. And of course famous bands like the Beatles and INXS deliberately spelled their names in clever and unusual ways.

Exploring menus

Once children have mastered the common GPCs in English they may be puzzled by unfamiliar grapheme–phoneme correspondences, especially in words which are in common usage in English but have foreign origins such as *ciabatta, jalfrezi, chow mein* and *pizza*. Menus can be a good resource for exploring such words. It is important that children recognise that although GPCs may be unusual to them, they are common in some other languages and that each phoneme in all words is represented by a grapheme.

Nonsense words

Sharing poems like 'The Jabberwocky' and stories like *The BFG* introduces children to invented words and makes discussion about pseudo words easier. Although there is much scepticism about the inclusion of pseudo words in the Phonics Screening Test, there is no indication at the time of writing that this element will be removed, so children in Year 1 need to be aware that they can use their decoding strategies to read invented vocabulary.

Word investigations

As children read more widely, they encounter more unusual grapheme–phoneme correspondences. Encourage them to use dictionaries to try to find other words with the same GPCs, for example: *sugar, sure; who, whole; want, wander, wash; work, word, worth.*

Other displays

In Year 1 the National Curriculum requires children to be able to:

• spell the days of the week;

• name the letters of the alphabet;

• name the letters of the alphabet in order;

• use letter names to distinguish between alternative spellings of the same sound.

Your classroom should, therefore, include a display of the alphabet, which can be seen easily by everyone and children should learn to say and sing the alphabet. Avoid placing this around the top of your classroom wall; it is common to use the alphabet frieze just below the ceiling. Many children do not look up this high and so rarely acknowledge its presence, never mind using it to support reading and writing. The frieze should, if possible, be just above eye height – and sitting eye height where this can be done – so that it is always within eye vision when children are at their tables or on the carpet.

Some phonics programmes introduce letters naming them by their sounds rather than their names, but children encounter letter names even before staring school (they may visit B & Q, see RAC and AA vans, watch BBC and ITV, etc.), so it may be confusing for them if they are not shown that letters have names and sounds. We saw one class become very confused when a student teacher told them that *e* (which she sounded as *e* in *bed*) made an 'e' sound in *red* and an 'ee' sound in *me* and *be*.

It would surely have been more logical to tell them that *e* (pronounced as the letter name) did this. Both Rose (2006) and Johnston and Watson (2007) advocate teaching letter names alongside letter sounds. Indeed, Johnston and Watson argue that *many of the letter names also provide a clue to the letter sounds* (p47) and produce a table (Table 12.6) which illustrates this.

Table 12.6 Letters where the names give clues to the sound of the letter

Name	Sound	Name	Sound
bee	/b/	eff	/f/
dee	/d/	ell	/l/
jay	/j/	em	/m/
kay	/k/	en	/n/
pea	/p/	ar	/r/
tea	/t/	ess	/s/
vee	/v/	ex	/x/
zed	/z/		

Source: Johnston and Watson (2007, p48).

The vital importance of reading aloud to children

An essential element of teaching children to read is sharing texts with them. Regular reading of stories and poems, as well as non-fiction texts, gives meaning to reading and shows children what they will be able to do as they develop their reading skills. It provides an opportunity to reinforce learning too, especially if cards are introduced with names of characters or story charts are displayed and labelled. Reading aloud to your class should not be restricted to an end-of-day treat, but should be an integral part of the school day. Crucially, when children hear a text read well, they can enjoy it in a way which might not be possible if they read it themselves, and they can hear how text sounds when read with expression and intonation.

Conclusion

In Chapter 1 we discussed the controversy surrounding systematic synthetic phonics epitomised by Davis's (2013) assertions that reading is not simply about mastering letter–sound correspondences, but is about the making of meaning, and that while phonics can help some children on their journey to becoming readers, it is not an approach that supports all children and, in particular, the able reader.

You should now be aware that while the National Curriculum and the Teachers' Standards make it a statutory requirement that you should teach using systematic synthetic phonics, there is actually more to teaching reading than phonics, and that the National Curriculum recognises this. The activities described in this chapter and in earlier chapters show that children can acquire phonemic awareness and an ability to decode and encode while engaging with meaningful activities, which also develop their comprehension skills and widen their vocabularies.

If you create a broad, rich language environment that places literacy at its heart, children will be able to develop both their phonic and comprehension skills and will develop a love of reading and writing.

Learning outcomes review

You have now explored ways in which phonics can be taught and you should be aware of a range of useful resources that can be used to support teaching and learning. You should have considered the school environment's potential for developing children's phonemic awareness.

Answers to football match activity (page 149)
There are lots of possibilities for matches, including:

- Asto<u>n</u> Villa v Bre<u>nt</u>ford

- <u>B</u>rentford v <u>B</u>righton

- <u>Ch</u>elsea v Ipswi<u>ch</u>

- <u>D</u>oncaster <u>R</u>overs v <u>B</u>rentfor<u>d</u>

- Fu<u>l</u>ham v <u>L</u>iverpool

References

Davis, A (2013) To read or not to read: Decoding synthetic phonics. *Impact: Philosophical Perspectives on Education Policy*, 20: 1–38.

Department for Education (DfE) (2013) *The National Curriculum in England: Framework Document*. London: DfE.

Johnston, R and Watson, J (2007) *Teaching Synthetic Phonics*. Exeter: Learning Matters.

Layton, L, Deeny, K and Tall, G (1998) A pre-school training program for children with poor phonological awareness: Effects on reading and spelling. *Journal of Research on Reading*, 21 (1): 36–52.

Rose, J (2006) *The Independent Review of the Teaching of Early Reading*. London: Department for Children, Schools and Families (DCSF).

For a range of lesson ideas and plans, see the Teachit website, which includes plans and resources produced by David Waugh and Jonathan Pye for some of the ideas described in this chapter. Available at: **www.teachitprimary.co.uk/literacy-resources** [accessed 4 April 2015].

Glossary

Adjacent consonants Consonants which appear next to each other in a word and can be blended together, e.g. *bl* in *blip*, *cr* in *crack* (note that the *ck* in *crack* is a digraph as the consonants come together to form a single sound or phoneme). Adjacent consonants are also referred to as 'consonant blends' in some phonics schemes.

Alliteration A sequence of words beginning with the same sound.

Analytic phonics Children learn to identify (analyse) the common phoneme in sets of words in which each word contains the phoneme that is the focus of the lesson. For instance, they might be asked to listen to the words *big, bag* and *bat* and decide in what ways the words sound alike. The focus is on identifying patterns in words and drawing analogies.

Blend A combination of letters where individual letters retain their sounds. The consonants retain their original sounds but are blended together, as in *slip, cram, blink* and *flop*.

Blending To draw individual sounds together to pronounce a word, e.g. /c/l/a/p/ blended together reads *clap*.

Cloze work Text which has missing words that students need to insert. Typically, every 10th, 11th, 12th word might be replaced by a line. Often students may choose different words to complete the text and they should be encouraged to work together to discuss logical possibilities.

Common exception words This is the term used in the 2013 English National Curriculum for common words with unusual grapheme–phoneme correspondences. These are the words which Letters and Sounds and other phonics programmes refer to as 'tricky words'. They are common words with phonic irregularities, e.g. *one, who, should*. See also *Tricky words*.

Consonant–vowel–consonant (CVC) words Children's early reading experiences will include words like *cat, dog, sit* and *pin*, which have single letters for each sound. Later, CVC words will include those with digraphs such as *ship, cheap* and *wish*.

Decodable Words which can be easily decoded using phonic strategies, e.g. *cat, dog, lamp*.

Decoding The act of translating graphemes into phonemes, i.e. reading.

Digraph Two letters which combine to make a new sound.

Encoding The act of transcribing units of sound or phonemes into graphemes, i.e. spelling.

Etymology   The origins of the formation of a word and its meaning.

Grapheme   A letter, or combination of letters, which represent a phoneme.

Homographs   Words which are spelled the same but pronounced differently according to context, e.g. 'That's a new world *record?*', 'I'll *record* The Archers and listen to it later'.

Homonyms   Words which are spelled and pronounced in the same way, but have different meanings, e.g. *bear*: 'I can't *bear* it any longer', 'The large *bear* growled'.

Homophones   Words which sound the same but have different spellings and meanings, e.g. *sea* and *see*, *their* and *there*.

Initial consonant   Consonant letter at the beginning of a word.

Kinaesthetic   Some people learn better using some form of physical (kinaesthetic) activity; hence the use of actions to accompany phonemes and graphemes in Jolly Phonics.

Long vowel phonemes   The long vowel sounds as in *feel* or *cold*.

Mnemonic   A device for remembering something, such as 'ee/ee/ feel the tree'.

Monosyllabic word   Word with one syllable, e.g. *big, black, club, drop*.

Morpheme   The smallest unit of meaning, e.g. *help* is a single morpheme, but we could add the suffix *-ful* to make *helpful*, and go on to add the prefix *un-* to make *unhelpful*, which has three morphemes.

Multi-sensory   Using a broad range of senses (hearing, seeing, feeling, moving).

Onset   The onset is the part of the word before the vowel; not all words have onsets. In *brush*, *br* is the onset (but note that *br* is two sounds). *Add* and *up* do not have onsets (there is no consonant phoneme before the vowel).

Orthographic system   The spelling system of a language, i.e. the ways in which graphemes and phonemes relate to each other. The English orthographic system is more complex than many languages, since most phonemes can be represented by more than one grapheme.

Orthography   Standardised spelling – the sounds of a language represented by written or printed symbols.

Phoneme   The smallest single identifiable sound, e.g. the letters *ch* representing one sound.

Phonemic awareness   An understanding that letters can be sounded as phonemes and can be put together to create words.

Phonetics   The articulation and acoustic features of speech sounds. It explains the distinction between consonants and vowels and can help listeners identify the phonemic pattern of words.

Phonological awareness The ability to perceive, recall and manipulate sounds.

Prefix Morpheme or affix placed before a word to modify its meaning, e.g. *dis-* in *dislike*, *de-* in *defrost*.

Rhyme Words that sound the same but do not necessarily share the same spelling.

Rime The rime of a word is the vowel and the rest of the syllable, e.g. the rime in *black* is *-ack*; the rime in *flop* is *-op*.

Segmenting Splitting up a word into its individual phonemes in order to spell it, i.e. the word *pat* has three phonemes: /p/a/t/.

Split digraph Two letters, making one sound, e.g. *a-e* as in *cake*.

Suffix Morpheme or affix added to a word to modify its meaning, e.g. *-ful* in *hopeful*, *-ed in jumped*.

Syllable A unit of pronunciation having one vowel sound. This can be taught by identifying 'beats' in a word. Putting a hand flat underneath your chin and then saying a word can help, as every time the hand moves, it represents another syllable.

Synthetic phonics Synthetic phonics involves separating words into phonemes and then blending the phonemes together to read the word. This compares with analytic phonics in which segments or parts of words are analysed and patterns are compared with other words.

Tricky words When teaching systematic synthetic phonics, we refer to common words with phonic irregularities as 'tricky words', e.g. *once, was, could*. See also *Common exception words*.

Trigraph Three letters which combine to make a new sound.

Index

Note: Page numbers in **bold** refer to the Glossary.

active learning 6
activities *see* games and activities
adjacent consonants 52, **157**
adjectives 88, 119, 134
adverbs 122
alliteration 29, 153, **157**
alphabetic method 5
alphabets 4
Alphablocks 35, 40
analytic phonics 5, 6, **157**
antonyms 86
apostrophes 106–7, 109

Bald, J. 4
Barretta, G. 105
bead strings for blending 29
Bell, M. 128
best guess displays 17
blending 39, 76, **157**
   activities/tasks 44
   assisted blending 40–1
   bead strings 29
   independent blending 41–2
   Key Stage 2 support 47, 82
   learning to blend 40
   Reception 38–46
blends **157**
body gym 31
book corner 18–19
bound morphemes 87
Brooks, G. 6
Bullock Report (1975) 6

case studies
   alien puppets 43
   Key Stage 2 support 47
   reading vs spelling 79
   role play 43
   teaching phonemes to EAL children 35
Centre for Literacy in Primary Education
   (CLPE) 17
child-centred education 6
children's literature 18, 22, 42, 55
classroom ethos 15
Cleary, B. 108
cloze work 135
common exception words 77, 127, 130, **157**
   see also tricky words
common nouns, verbs, adjectives 88, 134
common words 129
compound words 87, 89, 94–5

content words 133–4
contractions 106–7
   common contractions 107
   Key Stage 2 support 110
   Year 2 99–100, 106–9, 111, 113
Corbett, E.T. 111
Corbett, O. 109
Cremin, T. *et al.* 18
Crystal, D. 103
CVC (consonant–vowel–consonant) words 33, 39, **157**
   Reception 38–46, 48

Dahl, R. 136
Davis, A. 11, 156
Dear Deer 105
decodable words and texts 21–2, 79, **157**
decoding 8–9, 76, **157**
decoding and encoding text
   Key Stage 2 support 82
   Year 1 75–82, 83
Department for Education 21
dictation 135
digraphs 50–1, 67, 148, **157**
   see also split digraphs
displays 16–17, 143, 145–6, 154–5
dots and dashes 52, 55, 70, 71, 78, 79

EAL children: teaching phonemes 35
Education Endowment Fund 47
Ehri, L. *et al.* 15
encoding 76, **157**
   see also decoding and encoding text
enunciation 52–3, 58
etymology 92, **157**

flash cards
   GPCs 20, 42
   using gestures 30
free morphemes 87
function words 133

Gaiman, N. 2
Gambrell, L.B. 18
games and activities 19–20
   alliteration 29, 153
   anagrams of high-frequency words 150–1
   for blending 44
   body gym 31
   cloze work 135
   deliberate misspellings 153
   dictation 135

games and activities *cont.*
  fishing 19
  football matches 149–50
  GPCs 54–6
  graphemes 55, 146, 147–9
  guess my word 151
  matching games 135, 149–50
  menus 153
  mnemonics 68, 77, 136, 138
  nonsense words 153–4
  outdoors 20, 135–6, 146
  phonics bingo 150
  rhymes 32, 135, 145, 151–3
  right or wrong snap 150
  shops 19, 144
  short games and activities 151
  for sounds 29, 30, 56, 68
  spelling tests 118, 120–1, 123, 138
  Twister 20
  visualisation strategies 137
  word investigations 154
  words and actions 137
Goodman, K. 7
Goswami, U. 4
Gough, P.B. 8
graded texts 21
grapheme activities
  grapheme cards 147–9
  grapheme flowers 55
  grapheme hopscotch 146
  graphemes on the wall 146
grapheme–phoneme correspondences (GPCs) 20, 127
  activities 54–6
  flash cards 20, 42
  'grotty graphemes' 77, 131–2
  Key Stage 2 support 62
  in other languages 153
  Reception 30–1
  wall displays 16–17
  Year 1 49–61, 62
graphemes 5, 50, **157**
guided reading 23, 32
Guthrie, J.T. 20

Hall, K. 7
Hallet, E. 24
Harrison-Palmer, R. 131
Hart, C. 59
hearing impairments 81
Hegley, J. see *Stanley's Stick*
heteronyms 133
high-frequency words 54, 150–1
homographs 103, **158**
homonyms 103–4, **158**
homophones **158**
  common homophones 101–2
  defined 100–1
  Key Stage 2 support 106
  near-homophones 101
  teaching 103

homophones *cont.*
  tricky words 132–3
  Year 2 99–106, 110–12
hornbooks 5
Huey, E.G. 6

ICT use 35–6
I'm and Won't, They're and Don't 108
Independent Review of the Teaching of Early Reading see Rose
  Review
initial consonants **158**

Johnston, R. 10, 87, 127, 154–5
Jolliffe, W. *et al.* 4, 67
Jolly Phonics 16, 30, 35, 53, 68
Jolly Phonics Readers 131–2

Key Stage 2 support
  blending 47, 82
  contractions 110
  decoding and encoding text 82
  GPCs 62
  homophones 106
  long vowel digraphs 73
  morphemes 96
  spelling 116, 124
  working with parents and carers 73
kinaesthetic learning **158**

Layton, N. see *Stanley's Stick*
letter names and sounds 154–5
Letters and Sounds 15, 17, 33, 39, 40, 45, 53–4, 116, 127
lexical approaches 5
listening comprehension 8–9
Literacy (journal) 10
literate environment 15–16, 42, 51
  class shop 144
  digraph shop 144
  displays 16–17, 143, 145–6, 154–5
  numbers 144–5
  postcards from teddy 143–4
  working walls 143
  see also physical environment
Lloyd-Jones, M. 130
long vowel digraphs
  Key Stage 2 support 73
  Year 1 64–72, 74
long vowel phonemes 66–8, **158**
'look and say' approach 6–7

McGuinness, D. 65
Marsh, J. 24
Masterson, J. *et al.* 129
Miskin, R. see *Read, Write, Inc.*
mnemonics 68, 76, 136, **158**
modelling 52
  blending 40–1
  reading 17, 23
  writing 17, 24, 32
monosyllabic words **158**

morphemes 87, **158**
  bound morphemes 87
  free morphemes 87
  Key Stage 2 support 96
  Years 1–2 85–95, 96–8
  see also prefixes; suffixes
Mr Thorne Does Phonics 35, 40
Mudd, N. 103
multi-sensory **158**

National Curriculum
  common exception words 77, 127
  elements of a reader 3
  homophones and contractions 99–100
  Reception 27–8, 38–9
  Simple View of Reading model 8
  spelling 17
  synthetic phonics 6
  Year 1 viii–ix, 21, 50, 51, 54, 64–5, 70, 75–6,
    85–6, 87, 127, 154
  Year 2 86, 89, 104, 114–15
  Years 3–4 89–90
Nelson English Skills 115
neurolinguistic programming (NLP) 137
nonsense words 43, 153–4
nouns, common 88, 134

OFSTED 18, 20
onsets 40, **158**
oral word building 29, 91, 92
orchestration models of reading 8
orthographic memory 58
orthographic system 65, **158**
orthography 65, **158**
Oxford Owl 79

parents' and carers' meetings
  Key Stage 1 51–4
  Key Stage 2 73
phoneme charts 68–9
phoneme frames 31
phonemes 5, 28, 50, **158**
  learning to use 28
  main lesson 34
  teaching EAL children 35
phonemic awareness 4, 28, **158**
  see also Reception: developing phonemic awareness
phonetics 35, **158**
phonically decodable text 21–2
phonics 1, 3, 4–5, 24
phonics approach 5, 10–11
phonics grapheme charts/wall display 16–17
phonics in context 14–15
  applying phonics in decodable text 21–2
  planned opportunities for reading 20–1
  planned opportunities for writing 23–4
  shared and guided reading 22–3, 32
  see also literate environment; physical environment
Phonics Screening Check 42, 43, 50, 55, 60, 79, 90

phonological awareness 4, 28, **158**
phonology 4
physical environment 16
  book corner 18–19
  class shops 144
  displays 16–17, 143, 145–6, 154
  outdoors 20, 135–6, 146
  phonics grapheme charts/wall display 16–17
  role play areas 17–18
  vocabulary cards 16
  see also games and activities
Plowden Report (1967) 6
prefixes 86–7, **159**
  see also Years 1–2: morphemes
Primary National Strategy 8
pseudo words 42–3, 90–1, 150
  alternative approach 60–1
  nonsense words 153–4
  real or pseudo words? 55–6
  Welcome to Alien School 59–60
puppets 17, 32, 43

quadgraphs 50–1

Read Write Inc. 16, 20, 33, 39, 40, 54, 68, 77, 79, 115,
  127, 131
reading
  comprehension viii–ix, 3
  defined 2
  guided reading 23, 32
  key factors in development 18
  modelling 17, 23
  National Curriculum viii–ix, 3, 6, 8
  planned opportunities 20–1
  shared reading 22–3, 32
  spelling code 4, 65–6, 128–9
  word reading viii, 3
  see also blending; teaching approaches
reading aloud to children 42, 155
reading schemes 22
Reception: beginning to read and write
  38–46, 48
  activities/tasks 44
  CVC words 39
  key focus: phonics and blending 39–43
  main lesson 45–6
Reception: developing phonemic awareness 27–8
  key focus 31–3
  learning to use phonemes 28
  main lesson: teaching phonemes 34
  oral and aural phonemic awareness 29–30
  relating phonemes to graphemes 30–1
  teaching phonemic awareness 32–3
  use of ICT 35–6
repetition 20, 33, 40
rhymes 32, 135, 145, 151–3, **159**
rimes 40, **159**
role play 43
role play areas 17–18

Roosevelt, T. 128
Rose Review 9, 10, 14, 142–3, 154

Schonell spelling lists 103
schwa 33, 40, 43, 52–3, 66
Searchlights Model of reading 8
segmenting 30, 76–7, 78, **159**
shared reading 22–3, 32
shared writing 17, 23–4
shops 19, 144
Simple View of Reading model 8–9
Simplified Spelling Society 128
Snow, C.E. *et al.* 21
sound activities
    and actions 68
    ball throwing for each sound 30
    finding the sound 56
    sound bags 29
Spanish 4
spelling
    best guess displays 17
    complex orthography 4, 65–6, 128–9
    Key Stage 2 support 116, 124
    Schonell spelling lists 103
    teaching strategies 115–16
    Year 2 114–23
    Years 3–4 77, 89–90
    see also grapheme–phoneme correspondences;
        segmenting
spelling tests 118, 120–1, 123, 138
split digraphs 68, 120, 148, **159**
Stanley's Stick 80–1
story maps 32
story sacks 32
Strong, J. 109
Stuart, M. *et al.* 8
Styles, M. 10
sub-lexical approaches 5, 7
suffixes 86–7, 90, **159**
    -ly 119, 122–3
    -y 119–21
    see also Years 1–2: morphemes
Support for Spelling 47, 116, 132
syllables **159**
synthetic phonics 5, 6, 40, **159**
    research evidence 10–11
systematic synthetic phonics 1, 10, 52

Talk for Writing website 110
teaching approaches 2–3
    historical perspective 5–7
    theoretic underpinnings 7–9
To, N. *et al.* 87
Torgerson, C.J. *et al.* 15
tricky words 54, 77, 126–40, **159**
    common exception words 77, 127, 130
    common words 129
    content words 133–4
    heteronyms 133

tricky words *cont.*
    homophones 132–3
    learning strategies 135–8
    spelling irregularities 128–9
    teachers' misconceptions 130
    teaching tricky words 77–8
trigraphs 50–1, 67, 148, **159**
Truss, L. 107
Tunmer, W.E. 8

UK Literacy Association (UKLA) 18, 43
un- 86, 92

verbs, common 88, 134
visualisation strategies 137
vocabulary cards 16

wall displays 16–17
Washtell, A. 6
Watson, J. 10, 87, 127, 154–5
Waugh, D. 131
Welcome to Alien School 59–60
whole language approach 7
whole word approach 6–7
word banks 82
writing
    displays of children's writing 16
    modelling writing 17, 24, 32
    planned opportunities 23–4
    shared writing 17, 23–4
Wyse, D. 10

Year 1: decoding and encoding text 75–82, 83
    key focus 76–9
    learning to segment and blend 76–7
    main lesson 80–1
    next lesson 82
    reading vs spelling 79
    tricky words 77–8
    using decodable texts in school 79
Year 1: GPCs main lesson 57–61
    learning the 'ee' sound 57–8
    assessment 58–9
    using nonsense/pseudo words 59–60
    reading place names 60–1
Year 1: grapheme–phoneme correspondences
        49–56, 62
    activities 54–6
    essential set-up 51
    key focus 50–1
    parents' and carers' meetings 51–3
    teaching sequences 53–4
    see also Year 1: GPCs main lesson
Year 1: long vowel digraphs 64–72, 74
    key focus 65–6
    main lesson: 'ae' sound 70–2
    spellings for long vowel phonemes 66–8
    teaching your class 68
    vowel phonemes 66

Years 1–2: morphemes 85–95, 96–8
    compound words 87, 89, 94–5
    main lesson 92–5
    morphemes defined 87
    need to teach 87–90
    prefixes and suffixes 86–7
    teaching your class 90–1
Year 2: contractions 99–100, 106–9, 111
    common contractions 107
    lesson: teaching contractions 108–9
    resources 113
Year 2: homophones 99–106, 110–12
    common homophones 101–2
    homographs and homonyms 103–4
    homophones and phonic knowledge 104

Year 2: homophones *cont.*
    homophones defined 100–1
    main lesson 105–6
    near-homophones 101
    resources 111–12
    teaching homophones 103
Year 2: phonics into spelling 114–23
    learning strategies 121
    main lesson: adding suffix -*y* 119–21
    next lesson: adding suffix -*ly* 119, 122–3
    teaching strategies 115–16
    teaching your class 116–18
    testing spelling 118, 120–1, 123
Years 3–4
    spelling 89–90